*Test Yourself in*

# EVIDENCE
# CIVIL PROCEDURE
# CRIMINAL PROCEDURE
# SENTENCING

*Test Yourself in*

# EVIDENCE
# CIVIL PROCEDURE
# CRIMINAL PROCEDURE
# SENTENCING

Thirteenth Edition

Inns of Court
School of Law

Institute of Law
City University, London

OXFORD
UNIVERSITY PRESS

OXFORD
UNIVERSITY PRESS

Great Clarendon Street, Oxford OX2 6DP

Oxford University Press is a department of the University of Oxford.
It furthers the University's objective of excellence in research, scholarship,
and education by publishing worldwide in

Oxford New York

Auckland Cape Town Dar es Salaam Hong Kong Karachi
Kuala Lumpur Madrid Melbourne Mexico City Nairobi
New Delhi Shanghai Taipei Toronto

With offices in

Argentina Austria Brazil Chile Czech Republic France Greece
Guatemala Hungary Italy Japan Poland Portugal Singapore
South Korea Switzerland Thailand Turkey Ukraine Vietnam

Oxford is a registered trade mark of Oxford University Press
in the UK and in certain other countries

Published in the United States
by Oxford University Press Inc., New York



British Library Cataloguing in Publication Data
Data available

Library of Congress Cataloging in Publication Data
Data available

Typeset by Laserwords Private Limited, Chennai, India
Printed in Great Britain by
Ashford Colour Press Limited, Gosport, Hampshire

ISBN 0–19–920548–5 978–0–19–920548–6

1 3 5 7 9 10 8 6 4 2

# CONTENTS

# INTRODUCTION

**PLEASE DO NOT ATTEMPT, OR EVEN READ, THE MULTIPLE CHOICE TEST QUESTIONS CONTAINED IN THIS BOOK UNTIL YOU HAVE READ THIS INTRODUCTION!**

## A. THE PURPOSE OF THE MULTIPLE CHOICE TESTS

It must be rare, on opening a book and turning to its first page, to be greeted by a command, albeit a polite command. However, there is a very good reason for such a command: that if you do embark upon testing yourself before you have read the following few pages on (a) the purpose of the multiple choice tests (MCTs), (b) the nature and format of the MCTs, (c) popular misconceptions, and (d) advice on taking the tests, then it is likely that you will simply defeat the purposes of this book.

The MCTs contained in this book have two purposes. The first is to enable you to test, with speed and accuracy, whether you have a sound working knowledge and comprehension of the main principles of law and procedure, and the leading cases, in Evidence, Civil Litigation, Criminal Litigation and Sentencing. The MCT questions used are directed at the general rules, the principal exceptions to those rules and the leading authorities. Wherever possible, they concentrate on the modern law and important decisions. They are not directed at narrow, antiquated, abstruse or esoteric points that a practitioner, or even a scholar, might properly need to look up. This explains why, as we shall see, each question has to be answered in just over 2 minutes and 34 seconds.

The second purpose is to enable you, after the test, to identify, with precision, your weaknesses, the gaps in your knowledge and understanding, so that you can revisit these areas and take appropriate remedial action.

## B. THE NATURE AND FORMAT OF THE MCTs

This book contains two MCTs, the Civil MCT and the Criminal MCT. In terms of style and difficulty, they closely resemble the MCTs conducted annually on the Bar Vocational Course at the Inns of Court School of Law.

Each of the MCTs comprises 70 questions, to be taken at one sitting. The Civil MCT incorporates questions on the subjects normally found in the syllabuses for courses in Civil Procedure and Civil Evidence. The subjects in question are set out in Appendix 5. The Criminal MCT incorporates questions on the subjects normally found in the syllabuses for courses in Criminal Procedure, Sentencing and Criminal Evidence. These subjects are also set out in Appendix 5. Neither MCT should be attempted until you have completed your studies in all of the subjects in question.

The 70 questions of each MCT have to be answered in 3 hours. This means that if you divide the time equally between the questions you will have just over 2 minutes and 34 seconds to answer each question.

The MCTs use the following headings to identify the subject matter of the various questions: CIVIL LITIGATION; CIVIL EVIDENCE; CRIMINAL LITIGATION AND SENTENCING; and CRIMINAL EVIDENCE. So, if you wish to complete only part or parts of the MCTS, for example, the Civil Evidence questions only, you should recalculate the length of the test by reference to the number of questions you intend to attempt.

*Format*

The questions in the MCTs contained in this book are always accompanied by four possible answers: [A], [B], [C] and [D]. You are required to select just one answer, the one that you think is correct/the best. You should record the answers you select on a separate question sheet (detachable from the inside back cover of this book), by putting a pencil line through [A], [B], [C] or [D]. (Pencils allow you to use an eraser and change your mind!)

The questions often take the form of a factual problem and conclude with a specific question, such as 'On these facts, what is the most appropriate advice to give to the client?' or 'On these facts, which of the following orders is the judge most likely to make?'. Questions of this kind are designed to test whether you are able to recognise the law or procedure appropriate to the given facts and/or whether you are able to apply the law to the facts and thereby identify the correct outcome.

Other questions take the form of a number of legal propositions, only one of which is correct or, as the case may be, incorrect, or ask about a specific point of law. Thus as to the former, the question may read, 'Which of the following propositions is CORRECT?' or 'Which of the following propositions is INCORRECT?'. As to the latter, the question may state a rule of law and then conclude, for example, 'Which of the following is NOT an exception to this general rule?'. Questions of this kind are designed to test your knowledge of the law.

Some questions combine both a factual scenario and a choice of legal propositions so that, after setting out the facts, the question may read, for example, 'Which of the following best describes the principles which the court should apply to these facts?'.

*Creation and validation*

The questions used in the MCTs in this book are of the same kind and of the same standard as those used for assessment on the Bar Vocational Course; indeed, many of the questions in this book were originally created for, and have in fact been used for, assessment on the course. However, you may well come to the erroneous conclusion that the questions in this book are easier than those used on the course if you fail to take the **Advice on Taking the Tests** proffered in this Introduction (see under **D.** below), in particular the advice to take the tests under examination conditions (which include a strict time limit and a ban on the use of books and other materials).

A lot of effort properly goes into the creation and validation of questions devised for use at the Inns of Court School of Law. Each question is thoroughly scrutinised by senior members of staff specialising in the subject in question and specialist practitioners. Every effort is made to ensure that each question is clear, unambiguous and fair, with only one correct answer and three incorrect answers.

After each MCT, the results are subjected to an item-by-item statistical analysis, to show the facility, selectivity and reliability of each question. Facility simply means the proportion of candidates who answered a question correctly. It indicates how easy or difficult a particular question was. Selectivity is a measure of the correlation between those who answer a particular question correctly and those who do well in the test overall. A high selectivity rating shows that most 'good' candidates have answered the question correctly. Reliability is a measure of the overall effectiveness of the question, the product of facility and selectivity. If there is an average facility and a high selectivity, the question is very reliable at differentiating between 'good' and 'bad' candidates.

Using this statistical information, it is possible to review, and if necessary amend, questions. For example, it may be desirable to amend or delete a question with an unduly high or low facility rating. Equally, it is important to revisit a question with an unduly low selectivity or reliability rating to see whether it contained some ambiguity or was otherwise misleading, which might explain why 'good' candidates were getting it wrong.

## C. MCTs – POPULAR MISCONCEPTIONS

*'MCTs are easier than traditional examinations'*

This view tends to be expressed by those who have never sat an MCT. By contrast, the experience of students who have taken MCTs, both at home and overseas, is that such tests are much more demanding than traditional examinations. There are three principal reasons for this.

First, MCTs allow examiners to cover the whole syllabus. For students who have been brought up on conventional examinations and who have adopted the 'question-spotting' approach, the MCT obviously comes as a very nasty shock!

Second, the MCT offers no scope for the candidate who would 'waffle'. In conventional examinations, some students, unaware or not too sure of the correct answers, will hedge their bets, setting out at length all such seemingly relevant legal knowledge as they possess, but making no real effort to apply the law, simply skirting around the central issues with deliberate equivocation. There is no scope for such tactics in the MCT: faced with four competing answers, only one of which is correct, you must nail your colours to the mast.

Third, there is the obvious pressure that comes from having to answer 70 questions at the rate of about 2 ½ minutes per question. This calls for the ability to analyse, digest and comprehend material at speed, before reaching a firm conclusion, only to move on to repeat the exercise in the next question, and so on.

*'MCT means multiple guess or passing by good luck'*

It is perfectly accurate to say that if you go into the examination room with no relevant knowledge at all and sit an MCT in which each question has four competing answers, then by the law of averages you *could* score 25%. However, the pass mark is usually more than double 25%. On the Bar Vocational Course, for example, a student who answers correctly 60% of all the questions set, will achieve a bare pass; in many jurisdictions, the percentage required to pass is much higher. Students relying on guesswork or Lady Luck simply do not pass. However, as will be stressed below, when you do not know, or are unsure about, the correct answer to a particular question, you *should* make an intelligent guess, because no mark is deducted for a wrong answer.

*'MCTs are inferior to traditional tests and examinations'*

The validity of this criticism depends upon what one is seeking to test or examine. Obviously the MCT is not an appropriate tool to test oral legal skills such as Advocacy or Negotiation, just as it would be an inappropriate means of testing the practical skills of a pianist or an airline pilot. Equally, it cannot test a student's *written* skills, whether in drafting a statement of case, writing a legal essay or answering a legal problem (although it is interesting to note, in passing, that there is a high degree of correlation between student results in MCTs and in other forms of testing that do involve oral performances and written work). However, experience shows that the MCT is an excellent vehicle for testing, with accuracy, powers of analysis and levels of knowledge and comprehension. MCTs have been used to test doctors at both undergraduate and postgraduate level, and in other disciplines, for many years. Moreover, there is no question of examiner bias.

*'MCTs cannot test the "grey areas"'*

This is simply incorrect! For every 'grey area' question, there can be a suitably 'grey area' answer. For example, if on a particular point the authorities conflict, the correct answer may simply read: 'The authorities are in conflict on this point.' (Note, however, that such wording may also be used for an incorrect answer, ie in a question on a point on which the authorities are not in conflict at all.) Another possibility, in 'grey areas', is to build a question around the facts of an important reported case, thereby testing whether a student knows of, and has understood, that case. That said, it is certainly true that it can be more demanding to set good MCT questions in 'grey areas', and for this reason they tend to be avoided, unless they concern important areas of the law.

## D. ADVICE ON TAKING THE TESTS

The purpose of the MCTs in this book is likely to be defeated unless you observe certain basic rules.

### *1. DO NOT ATTEMPT AN MCT UNTIL YOU HAVE COMPLETED YOUR STUDIES IN THE SUBJECTS COVERED*

The MCTs in this book are designed to be taken only *after* you have completed your studies in the subject areas covered and *before* you are formally examined in them.

### *2. TAKE THE MCT UNDER EXAMINATION CONDITIONS*

Make sure that you will have an *uninterrupted* period of 3 hours in which to complete the *whole test*. If you wish to complete only part or parts of either MCT, for example the Evidence questions only, you should recalculate the length of the test by reference to the number of questions you intend to attempt and the number of permitted minutes per question (roughly 2 minutes and 34 seconds). If you are working at home, tell any other residents that you do not wish to be disturbed, and turn off all telephones! Also remove from the room any relevant books or materials that you might be tempted to use. The MCT is a closed-book examination.

*3. USE THE ANSWER SHEET*

On starting the test, detach the appropriate Answer Sheet from the inside back cover of this book and read carefully the Instructions on that Answer Sheet.

*4. OBSERVE THE TIME LIMITS*

Observe the overall time limit and try to spend no longer than an average of about 2 ½ minutes on each question. You will doubtless find that some of the questions can be answered in less time, whereas others require slightly more time – the questions vary in length and difficulty. However, the overall time limit reflects the standard of the MCT as a whole, and should not be exceeded.

*5. READ ALL FOUR COMPETING ANSWERS TO EACH QUESTION BEFORE MAKING A SELECTION*

Whether a problem-type question or a propositions-type question, you should *always* look at all four competing answers before making a selection. There are three good reasons for doing so.

First, an answer may refer to another answer or answers. For example, the question may set out a judge's ruling on a particular point of law, and conclude, 'Which of the following reasons could justify the judge's ruling?'. [A] may then set out one reason and suggest that this *alone* could justify the ruling; [B] may set out a different reason and suggest that this *alone* could justify the ruling; and [C] may read: 'The reasons in both [A] and [B].'

Second, even when you are confident or relatively confident that you know the correct answer before you even look at the options on offer, and you are therefore tempted to simply select the 'correct' answer and to ignore the other answers, reading those other answers to check that they are indeed incorrect is the best way of confirming your initial selection.

Third, there may well be occasions when you are unsure as to the correct answer. In these circumstances, it is often possible to identify the correct answer by the process of eliminating others that you know to be incorrect. Often you will find that the question-setter has included one answer that is quite obviously incorrect and another that is also incorrect, although not quite so obviously, thereby reducing the effective choice from four to two. The two remaining answers will test whether you have understood the legal principle in question.

### *6. TREAT THE EXAMINERS AS IF INFALLIBLE*

If your initial reaction, on reading a particular question and the four competing answers, is that you need more factual information before you can select the correct answer, or that there are two correct answers, or that the correct answer seems to have been omitted, quickly swallow your pride and re-read the question to see if there is something that you have missed or the importance of which you failed to take note on the first reading. If, having re-read the question and answers, you remain convinced that you need more information, or that there are two correct answers, or no correct answer, then select the answer that, in your opinion, gets nearest to being correct or is the best from which you have to make a choice. Remember that most of the questions have been thoroughly scrutinised by specialist academics and practitioners and statistically tested in terms of their selectivity and reliability (see above).

### *7. IF NECESSARY, MAKE AN INTELLIGENT GUESS*

As already explained, multiple choice does not mean multiple guess or passing by good luck. However if, having read a particular question, you do not know the correct answer and are unable to eliminate all of the incorrect answers, then you *should* make an intelligent guess, and move on. As previously noted, you do *not* lose a mark for a wrong answer.

### *8. MARK YOUR PERFORMANCE*

After you have completed the MCT – and probably after a break of suitable length – you will want to mark your performance. You will find the correct answers to the Civil MCT and the Criminal MCT listed in Appendix 1 and Appendix 2 respectively. Award yourself one mark for each question that you have answered correctly. If you have selected one of the other three answers to the question, selected more than one answer, or not made a selection at all, you should *not* subtract a mark – you simply gain no mark for that question. You may then rate your overall performance according to the following table.

| Number of questions answered correctly | Comment |
|---|---|
| 0–41 | A performance ranging from the awful to the weak. At best, on 41, you are showing insufficient knowledge and comprehension in 41% of all subjects tested. |
| 42–53 | A performance ranging from one of bare competence to competence. You are showing insufficient knowledge and comprehension in c. 24–40% of all subjects tested. |
| 54–61 | A performance ranging from the very competent to the all but outstanding. You are showing insufficient knowledge and comprehension in c. 13–23% of all subjects tested. |
| 62–70 | An outstanding performance. You are showing insufficient knowledge and comprehension in less than 12% of all subjects tested. |

### *9. REVIEW YOUR PERFORMANCE*

After you have marked your performance, take a break! You need to be fully refreshed before you embark upon the most important part of the exercise, namely the review of your performance by reference to the note-form answers to the questions of the Civil MCT and the Criminal MCT, which you will find in Appendix 3 and Appendix 4 respectively. Thorough review is important because it allows you to identify with precision the gaps in your knowledge and understanding of the law with a view to further work or revision.

Look at *all* of the note-form answers, not just those to the questions which you got wrong. By looking at the answers to the questions that you answered correctly, you will usually confirm your understanding of the law. Sometimes, however, you may discover that, although your answer was in fact correct, your reasoning was defective. Equally, you need to know the reasons for answers to questions to which you could only make an inspired guess.

# THE CIVIL MCT

# [TIME LIMIT: 3 HOURS]

## CIVIL LITIGATION

**1.** The Court of Appeal in *Anton Piller KG v Manufacturing Processes Ltd* (1976) laid down a number of preconditions for the making of a search order. Three of the four following propositions accurately reflect conditions stated by the Court of Appeal. One does not. Which one?

[**A**] There must be clear evidence that the defendants have in their possession incriminating documents or things, and that there is a real possibility that they may destroy such material before any application on notice can be made.
[**B**] The damage, actual or potential, must be very serious for the claimant.
[**C**] The claim must concern the infringement of intellectual property rights.
[**D**] The claimant must show an extremely strong prima facie case on the merits.

**2.** Julia issued a claim form not indorsed with her particulars of claim in the High Court against Rick alleging breach of contract. The only remedy she seeks is specific performance of the contract. More than a month has passed since the claim form was served and neither party has done anything since then. Julia wants advice about entering judgment in default at this stage. Which one of the following propositions is CORRECT?

[**A**] Judgment in default is not possible because Julia's claim is for equitable relief, which falls outside the rules allowing the entry of judgment in default.
[**B**] Judgment in default is not possible because Julia's claim for specific performance should have been commenced by a Part 8 claim, to which the default judgment procedure does not apply.
[**C**] Judgment in default can be entered because the time for acknowledging service has expired and Rick has not returned the acknowledgment of service form.
[**D**] Judgment in default cannot be entered at this stage because Julia has not served her particulars of claim.

**3.** Rachel wishes to commence proceedings to claim the cost of repairs to her car in the sum of £2,200 and compensation for minor bruising sustained in a road accident. Your instructing solicitor has asked for your advice on the nature of the proceedings if they are contested by the defendant. Which one of the following is the advice you should give?

[**A**] The claim is likely to be a High Court small-claims-track case.
[**B**] The claim is likely to be a county court small-claims-track case.
[**C**] The claim is likely to be a High Court fast-track case.
[**D**] The claim is likely to be a county court fast-track case.

**4.** Eric builds a house for Kate. The house is defective. Kate sues Eric in the High Court. Eric says that the defects were due to bad workmanship by George, one of his subcontractors. Eric also alleges that George damaged some of his equipment. Eric issues an additional claim under Part 20 against George claiming an indemnity in respect of any damages awarded against him together with damages for the damaged equipment. Kate's claim against Eric is struck out for breach of an 'unless' order. Which one of the following statements is CORRECT?

**[A]** Both of Eric's claims against George (for the indemnity and for the damaged equipment) fall with Kate's claim against Eric, and so Eric will have to issue a Part 7 claim against George.

**[B]** Both of Eric's claims against George continue together independently of the claim brought by Kate.

**[C]** Eric's claim for the indemnity falls with Kate's claim, but his claim for the damage to his equipment continues independently of the claim brought by Kate.

**[D]** Both of Eric's claims against George continue, but the court will order separate trials because the remedies claimed are not of the same or a similar nature.

**5.** Marine Fish Ltd, a large trawler concern operating around Dover, has suffered severe losses due, it says, to the dumping of phosphates off the French coast by the large French soap powder producers, Savon SA. Assume that there is a good cause of action against the defendant, that the tort was committed in France and that Marine Fish Ltd suffered damage in England. Marine Fish Ltd wish to know whether it can pursue a claim against Savon SA within the jurisdiction.

Which one of the following statements is CORRECT?

**[A]** Since Savon SA is domiciled in France, under the Jurisdiction Regulation (Council Regulation (EC) No. 44/2001) the claim must be pursued in France.
**[B]** Since the tort was committed on French territory, the claim must be pursued in France.
**[C]** Since the damage was sustained in England, Marine Fish Ltd should seek permission to serve the claim out of the jurisdiction.
**[D]** Since the damage was sustained in England, Marine Fish Ltd can sue Savon SA in France or in England. The choice is with Marine Fish Ltd. If it chooses to sue within the jurisdiction no permission is required to serve the claim.

**6.** Which one of the following is an INCORRECT statement about the practice relating to standard disclosure in a multi-track claim?

**[A]** The parties should provide each other with a disclosure statement signed by their solicitors.
**[B]** The items to be disclosed include anything on which information is recorded, and are not restricted to written documents.
**[C]** The parties are under a duty to make a reasonable search for documents that ought to be disclosed to the other side.
**[D]** The parties should serve each other with lists of documents within the time laid down in case management directions by the court.

**7.** Gillian has recently been served with proceedings brought by a government department making a claim based on the provisions of a recent statute. You have advised Gillian that she may have an argument that the statute is incompatible with the provisions of the European Convention on Human Rights. How should you first raise this human rights point in this claim?

**[A]** By issuing an application notice seeking to raise the human rights point as a preliminary issue.
**[B]** By setting the human rights point out in Gillian's defence.
**[C]** By including the human rights point in your skeleton argument, which has to be served and filed in advance of the trial.
**[D]** By raising the human rights point in the course of oral argument at the trial.

**8.** Siew Leng has brought a claim against Martha. Shortly after the claim was allocated to the multi-track, Siew Leng sent a written offer (complying with any relevant rules), without prejudice save as to costs, under which she offered to settle the claim for £65,000. This was rejected by Martha. At trial today, judgment has been given to Siew Leng with damages assessed at £90,000. Which one of the following best describes the relevance of Siew Leng's offer?

**[A]** It is irrelevant to any decision that needs to be made by the court, because the offer was made without prejudice.
**[B]** The offer shows that Siew Leng has been successful at trial, which means that Martha should be ordered to pay Siew Leng's costs of the entire proceedings.
**[C]** As judgment is for more than Siew Leng's offer, the court has a discretion to award costs on the indemnity basis and to award additional interest on damages and costs from the expiry of the period for accepting the offer.
**[D]** The court has a discretion whether to take Siew Leng's offer into account when considering the question of costs. It is most likely to exercise that discretion by ordering Martha to pay Siew Leng's standard basis costs from the expiry of the period for accepting the offer.

**9.** You are instructed on behalf of Howard, who has been served with a claim form and an interim injunction made without notice restraining him from publishing an allegedly defamatory article about Agnes.

Howard has served a witness statement asserting that the contents of the draft article are true, and has applied to discharge the injunction. Which one of the following propositions best describes the principle that will be applied on the application?

[**A**] Provided there is a serious issue on the question of defamation, the court will consider the adequacy of damages to either side and the balance of convenience.

[**B**] As Howard has stated in his witness statement that he intends to plead justification, the injunction should ordinarily be discharged to protect freedom of speech unless the alleged libel is obviously untrue.

[**C**] As Howard has stated in his witness statement that he intends to plead justification, the injunction will be discharged to protect freedom of speech, and the court will not investigate the veracity of what Howard says in his witness statement.

[**D**] As the application is likely finally to dispose of the dispute, the injunction will be continued only if the merits of Agnes's case are overwhelming.

**10.** Robert moored his yacht 'Swift' alongside a quay at 7.30 am in a small North Wales village. When he reached the top of the steps he noticed an artist painting the harbour. He then set out for the nearby town with Miles, his crewman, for stores. On their return at 11 am they were aghast to find the 'Swift' severely damaged after a collision. There were, when they returned, several fairly large fishing vessels in the harbour which had not been there at 7.30. The artist was still painting. When Robert asked if he had seen what happened, the artist said that it was against his principles to tell tales on anyone. At the post office Robert found out that the artist was Vincent Morgan, and that he lived in the village. No one else seems to have seen anything. You are instructed to advise Robert.

Which one of the following is the most appropriate advice to give him?

**[A]** That a pre-action application notice be issued against Vincent requesting disclosure pursuant to the Supreme Court Act 1981, s 33(2).

**[B]** That a claim be issued seeking a *Norwich Pharmacal* order against Vincent.

**[C]** That no pre-action disclosure is available against Vincent because he is protected by the privilege against self-incrimination.

**[D]** That no pre-action disclosure is available against Vincent because he is a mere witness.

**11.** David, a tenant, made out a cheque for £6,000 in favour of Peter, his landlord, in respect of rent due. On presentation, the cheque was dishonoured and accordingly Peter issued a county court claim against David with particulars of claim claiming £6,000 due on the cheque. David has filed a defence and counterclaimed for damages of £4,000 for breach by Peter of a covenant in the lease to carry out certain repairs to the rented property (which has diminished the rental value of the property). Peter has now applied for summary judgment under CPR Part 24.

Which one of the following orders is the district judge most likely to make?

**[A]** Dismissal of the application.
**[B]** Judgment for Peter in the sum of £6,000.
**[C]** Judgment for Peter limited to the sum of £2,000 with the application refused as to the remainder of Peter's claim (ie, £4,000).
**[D]** Judgment for Peter in the sum of £6,000 but with a stay of execution in respect of £4,000 of the £6,000 pending the trial of the counterclaim.

**12.** Isaac is claiming damages from his employer, Highbury Upholstery Ltd, in respect of a respiratory disease he alleges he contracted from involuntary inhalation of products used in the factory where he works. Eighteen months ago Isaac made an application to the Department for Work and Pensions (DWP) for industrial disablement benefit. This involved completing an application form and attending a medical board, which completed a written report form. Highbury intend to apply for disclosure of these documents from the DWP.

Which one of the following propositions is CORRECT?

**[A]** Highbury can only obtain an order for disclosure against the DWP after proceedings are commenced, the order being sought by application notice.
**[B]** Highbury can only obtain an order for disclosure against the DWP after proceedings are commenced, the order being sought by issuing a Part 8 claim.
**[C]** Highbury can first obtain an order for disclosure against the DWP before the substantive proceedings start, the order being sought by issuing a Part 8 claim.
**[D]** Highbury cannot obtain an order against the DWP for disclosure (other than by witness summons) because Isaac's claim is not for personal injuries.

**13.** Mark is injured in an accident at his place of work. He alleges that the machine in question was badly maintained and he believes that there have been similar accidents before. He brings county court proceedings against his employer. In disclosure by lists, no mention is made in the employer's list of documents of accident reports relating to the earlier accidents involving the machinery. In these circumstances which one of the following is the application you would advise Mark to make?

**[A]** An order compelling the employer to attend before the district judge for cross-examination as to the documents in his possession, custody or control.
**[B]** An order that the employer make a further and better list of documents.
**[C]** An order that the employer verify his list of documents by affidavit.
**[D]** An order for specific disclosure.

**14.** Which one of the following statements is CORRECT?

**[A]** If a High Court claim is served outside the jurisdiction pursuant to the provisions of the Jurisdiction Regulation (Council Regulation (EC) No. 44/2001), judgment in default may be entered without permission once the extended period for acknowledging service has expired.
**[B]** Where a judgment is entered in default less than 14 days after service of the particulars of claim, it will be set aside on an application by the defendant as of right.
**[C]** On an application to set aside a regular judgment entered in default, the primary consideration is the defendant's explanation for allowing the judgment to be entered.
**[D]** Judgment in default can be entered only when the defendant fails to acknowledge service within 14 days after the deemed date of service of the claim form.

**15.** Where the court applies the guidelines in *American Cyanamid v Ethicon* (1975) on an application for an interim injunction, which one of the four following propositions best describes the degree to which the claimant must establish the merits of his case?

**[A]** The claimant must show that there is a serious issue to be tried.
**[B]** The claimant must show a strong prima facie case that his rights have been infringed.
**[C]** The claimant must show that his claim is more likely to succeed than fail at the trial.
**[D]** The claimant must show, on the balance of probabilities, that there is no defence to the claim.

**16.** In proceedings brought by a Part 8 claim, when is the claimant required to serve the defendants with his or her written evidence in support?

**[A]** At the same time as the Part 8 claim form is served on each defendant.
**[B]** On each defendant within 14 days of that defendant acknowledging service.
**[C]** On each defendant at least 14 days before the day listed for the first Master's appointment.
**[D]** After the Master's appointment in accordance with directions made by the Master on that appointment.

**17.** Which one of the following propositions, all of which relate to applications for summary judgment under CPR Part 24, is INCORRECT?

**[A]** Such an application can be made in any claim in either the High Court or county courts, subject to a limited number of exceptions.
**[B]** Such an application can be made for an injunction.
**[C]** Where a respondent to such an application intends to rely on evidence in opposition to the application, his evidence should be served on the applicant at least seven clear days before the return day.
**[D]** Where a respondent to such an application pays money into court in compliance with a conditional order, such money remains part of the respondent's general assets if he subsequently goes bankrupt.

**18.** You have been asked to advise Dennis, who has been served with a claim form and particulars of claim seeking damages for breach of contract. Dennis does not accept that he was in breach, but has agreed with the view you expressed in conference that on the evidence there is a risk that he will be found liable. Your instructing solicitor is hopeful that proposals can be made that will lead to the claim being settled in the near future, but that it will be a few weeks before an offer can be made. Which one of the following is the best advice to give Dennis?

[**A**] Enter into negotiations with the claimant's solicitors, indicating in without-prejudice correspondence that an offer to settle will be made in the next few weeks.
[**B**] File an acknowledgment of service, and then issue an application notice seeking an extension of time for filing the defence.
[**C**] File a defence, and ask for a stay for negotiation in the allocation questionnaire.
[**D**] File a defence, and then issue an application notice seeking an order for a stay of the claim to allow time for negotiations.

**19.** For some years James has purported to exercise a right of way along a path over Lynn's land. Hearing that Lynn intends to build an outbuilding across the path, James has applied on notice for an interim injunction. Which one of the following propositions best describes the relevance or otherwise of the fact that the building work has not yet commenced?

[**A**] It has no direct relevance to the question whether the injunction should be granted, apart from being part of the factual background.
[**B**] Its only relevance is as to whether damages would be an adequate remedy for either party.
[**C**] It is likely to be the decisive factor if the other factors bearing on the convenience of granting the injunction are evenly balanced.
[**D**] Its only relevance is in deciding whether the proposed injunction is mandatory or prohibitory.

**20.** Claude owns a large international pharmaceutical business of long standing based in Switzerland. Most of his trade is with the Far East, although he has a small number of dealings in England. Theresa has commenced proceedings in London against Claude claiming £640,000 under a contract of sale governed by English law. A fully pleaded defence was served five weeks ago alleging that the goods delivered were not of the required quality. Insurance monies in respect of another matter have recently become payable to Claude in London. One hour ago Claude received a telex in Switzerland to the effect that an order had been obtained by Theresa from Mr Justice Green restraining him from removing any of his assets from England, save in so far as they exceed £640,000, until judgment or further order. His London solicitors are now consulting you by telephone. Which one of the following is the best advice to give Claude?

**[A]** To press the insurance company for payment before they are notified of the order.

**[B]** To apply for the order to be discharged on the ground that, proceedings having been served, notice of the application to Mr Justice Green should have been given to Claude.

**[C]** To apply for the order to be discharged on the ground that such an order cannot be made after service of a fully pleaded defence.

**[D]** To apply for the order to be discharged on the ground that Claude is not the sort of defendant against whom such an order should be made.

**21.** You are instructed to advise Sunil, who wishes to claim damages from Allpurpose Machines Plc ('AMP') for defective performance of a contract to supply and install an automated packaging machine at Sunil's factory. The alleged breach of contract occurred four years ago. Sunil wishes to commence proceedings as soon as possible. Which one of the following should you include in your advice?

[**A**] This claim is governed by the Commercial Litigation Pre-Action Protocol, so Sunil will have to follow the procedure laid down by the Protocol, which includes sending a letter of claim to AMP and allowing AMP three months to investigate and respond to the claim.

[**B**] This claim is not governed by any pre-action protocol, but Sunil must follow a reasonable pre-action procedure, which should include sending a letter of claim to AMP and allowing AMP a reasonable time to investigate and respond to the claim.

[**C**] This claim is not governed by any pre-action protocol, so there are no restrictions on commencing proceedings, which can be issued immediately.

[**D**] Because the limitation period has nearly expired, Sunil will be permitted to issue proceedings immediately. If AMP need time to investigate the claim or to negotiate, that can be dealt with by the court granting a reasonable stay of proceedings after they have been issued.

**22.** At an earlier stage in proceedings between Peter and Karen a direction was made for the exchange of witness statements, which was due to take place eight months ago. No trial date has been fixed. Karen's witness statements were ready for exchange on the due date. Peter has failed to respond to letters from Karen's solicitors asking for the exchange to take place. Neither party has disclosed its witness statements. Karen has now applied to strike out Peter's claim for non-compliance with the direction. Which one of the following is the most likely approach that will be adopted by the court?

**[A]** The claim is unlikely to be struck out unless it is no longer possible to have a fair trial.
**[B]** Eight months is likely to be regarded as protracted delay, so the claim is likely to be struck out.
**[C]** As no trial date has been fixed it is most likely that Karen's application will be dismissed.
**[D]** As Karen has not disclosed her witness statements, her application is very likely to be dismissed.

**23.** Which one of the following provides a ground for making an order for an interim payment?

**[A]** The defendant being insured.
**[B]** The claimant establishing a genuine need for money arising out of the consequences of the defendant's alleged conduct.
**[C]** Judgment having been entered for damages to be decided by the court.
**[D]** The court being satisfied that the claim is for a substantial sum of money taking into account any set-off or counterclaim.

**24.** Graham has served Henry with a county court claim form with particulars of claim attached. You have calculated the deemed date of service as 1 December 2006. On 8 December 2006 Henry filed the acknowledgment of service form with the county court and intends to defend the claim. You have been asked to advise Henry on the timetable for what should happen next. Which one of the following is your advice?

**[A]** Henry must file and serve a defence by 22 December 2006.
**[B]** Henry must file and serve a defence by 29 December 2006.
**[C]** Graham will be able to apply for a default judgment on or after 15 December 2006.
**[D]** Graham will need to apply for the claim to be allocated to a case management track by 22 December 2006.

**25.** Richard, who owns a garden centre, purchased some catalogues from Barchester Printing Ltd. The catalogues, which were supplied in July 2000, were very poorly printed. Richard served proceedings together with his particulars of claim in May 2006. In August 2006 Barchester served a defence alleging that the contract was made not with it but with Barchester Printing (1982) Ltd, a different company but with the same registered office. It is now December 2006 and Richard wishes to amend his proceedings by substituting Barchester Printing (1982) Ltd for Barchester Printing Ltd. Which one of the following CORRECTLY describes the principle that will be applied by the court?

**[A]** Richard's application may be granted if Barchester Printing Ltd was named in the claim form in mistake for the new party.
**[B]** Richard's application may be granted because the companies have the same registered office.
**[C]** Richard's application cannot be granted because the court has no jurisdiction to allow such an amendment once the limitation period has expired.
**[D]** Richard's application cannot be granted unless he can show that Barchester deliberately tried to mislead him as to the identity of the contracting party.

**26.** On an assessment of costs on the standard basis, which one of the following principles should be applied?

**[A]** There should be allowed all costs except in so far as they are of an unreasonable amount or have been unreasonably incurred, any doubts being resolved in favour of the receiving party.
**[B]** The court shall have an unfettered discretion as to the items of expenditure to be allowed and as to the amount to be allowed in respect of such items.
**[C]** The party paying the costs shall not be ordered to pay more than such amount (if any) as is reasonable having regard to the financial circumstances of all the parties and their conduct in connection with the dispute.
**[D]** There should be allowed a reasonable and proportionate amount in respect of all costs reasonably incurred, any doubts being resolved in favour of the paying party.

**27.** After judgment has been obtained in the county court, which one of the following methods of enforcement is not executed by the bailiff?

**[A]** Seizure and sale of the judgment debtor's goods in satisfaction of a money judgment.
**[B]** Seizure of listed and identified goods for delivery to the claimant.
**[C]** Attaching a debt due from a third party to the judgment debtor so that the third party is required to pay the debt direct to the judgment creditor.
**[D]** Removal of persons from land and giving possession to the claimant.

**28.** In June 2003 your client, Julia, was injured at work through the negligence of her employers, Cannonfodder Ltd ('CF'), in circumstances where her cause of action accrued immediately. She consulted your instructing solicitors in November 2004. Proceedings were issued against CF in May 2006. As negotiations had by then reached a sensitive stage, your instructing solicitors decided that service should be delayed pending the outcome of negotiations. They did not notify CF's solicitors that proceedings had been issued.

It is now December 2006, negotiations have broken down, and the claim form has still not been served. CF's solicitors have indicated that CF will defend the claim, inter alia on the grounds that it is now too late for Julia to serve the claim form. You have advised Julia that the period of validity of the claim form has expired. Which one of the following reflects the additional advice you should give Julia?

**[A]** Once more than four months have elapsed since the claim form was issued, the court has no power to grant an extension to the period of validity.

**[B]** That there are strong grounds for seeking an order renewing the claim form for a sufficient period to allow for service.

**[C]** That the claim form should not be renewed, and the court has no power under the Limitation Act 1980, s 33 on these facts to direct that the primary limitation period shall be disapplied if a second claim form were to be issued.

**[D]** That the claim form should not be renewed, but a second claim form may be issued in respect of Julia's injuries, and an application under the Limitation Act 1980, s 33 may be made with some prospects of success for a direction that the primary limitation period shall be disapplied.

**29.** Rupert brings High Court proceedings against Gaston claiming damages in respect of an alleged breach of a contract made in England. Gaston has substantial assets in England, but is domiciled in Belgium. Belgium, like England and Wales, is subject to the Jurisdiction Regulation (Council Regulation (EC) No. 44/2001). Rupert wishes to obtain a freezing injunction against Gaston. Which one of the following statements, regarding the power of the High Court to grant a freezing injunction, is CORRECT?

**[A]** A freezing injunction can never be granted against a defendant who is domiciled in another European Union country.
**[B]** It is irrelevant to the grant or refusal of a freezing injunction that the defendant is domiciled in another European Union country.
**[C]** A freezing injunction can only be granted against a defendant who is domiciled in another European Union country if a court possessing jurisdiction to grant that country's equivalent of a freezing injunction first gives its consent.
**[D]** The relative ease of enforcement of judgments against a defendant domiciled in another European Union country is a factor to be taken into account in deciding whether or not to grant a freezing injunction.

**30.** Magic Makeup, a South African company, contracted to buy a quantity of lipsticks from Daisy Bell Products Inc, an American company incorporated in New York. By its terms, English law is to govern the contract. The contract also contains a jurisdiction clause which states 'the High Court in London shall have jurisdiction to determine any disputes arising out of this contract'. Daisy Bell Inc have considerable assets in England. Magic Makeup now want to sue Daisy Bell for breach of contract in the High Court in London. How should Magic Makeup be advised?

**[A]** That Magic Makeup have an absolute right to use the English courts by virtue of the fact that the contract confers jurisdiction on the High Court in London.
**[B]** That Magic Makeup should seek permission from the High Court to serve a claim on Daisy Bell in the USA.
**[C]** That Magic Makeup can serve a High Court claim form on Daisy Bell in the USA without permission.
**[D]** That Magic Makeup will have to sue Daisy Bell in New York, as, due to the fact that Daisy Bell are incorporated there, those courts have sole jurisdiction.

**31.** Winston is suing Laura for damages for an alleged breach of contract committed three years ago. Laura served Winston with a request for further information of the particulars of claim seven months ago, and the Master made an order five months ago requiring Winston to provide that information within the next 21 days. Winston has not yet served the information. Which one of the following orders is most likely to be made upon an application by Laura?

**[A]** An unless order with a sanction in default in respect of the further information.
**[B]** An order dismissing the claim on the grounds of inordinate and inexcusable delay.
**[C]** An order striking out the particulars of claim as an abuse of the process of the court.
**[D]** An order that the claim be discontinued.

**32.** Jane is suing her employer for damages following an accident when her arm was trapped in the doors of a lift at work. You are instructed to advise Jane whether it is possible to obtain copies of her employer's witnesses' statements before trial. Which one of the following CORRECTLY states the situation?

**[A]** There is jurisdiction to order the exchange of witnesses' statements only in the specialist courts, such as the Commercial and Admiralty Courts, of the High Court.
**[B]** Mutual exchange of witnesses' statements is one of the directions usually made at the allocation stage or case management conference in both the High Court and the county court.
**[C]** Whether the claim is proceeding in the High Court or the county court, requiring an exchange of witnesses' statements is only possible if an order is made on an application to the court.
**[D]** Witnesses' statements are covered by legal professional privilege, and it is not possible to obtain an order for the disclosure of the other side's witnesses' statements.

**33.** A county court circuit judge gives final judgment in the sum of £26,000 in a claim allocated to the multi-track based on an alleged breach of contract. If the defendant wishes to appeal, to which one of the following should the appeal be brought?

**[A]** A High Court judge in private.
**[B]** A High Court judge sitting in public.
**[C]** The Court of Appeal.
**[D]** The Divisional Court.

**34.** Paul has made a personal injuries claim that has been allocated to the multi-track. Last year he disclosed a report on his injuries by Mr Brown, a consultant surgeon. More recently Paul has decided to change experts, and earlier this year he disclosed a more favourable report by Mr Green. The case has now come on for trial. Mr Green has been called for Paul, but Mr Brown has not. Mr Brown's report corresponds with a report from Mr White prepared for the defendant. Paul objects to the defendant putting in evidence Mr Brown's report. How should the judge rule on the defendant's application to adduce Mr Brown's report?

**[A]** That it is inadmissible by virtue of the implied undertaking not to use the report without the consent of the party who disclosed it, in this case, Paul.
**[B]** That it is inadmissible without Paul's consent by virtue of the confidential relationship between doctor and patient.
**[C]** That it is protected by legal professional privilege, unless Paul waives the privilege.
**[D]** That it is admissible regardless of Paul's consent.

**35.** You are instructed by Kurall plc, a company that manufactures drugs, against whom proceedings have been commenced in the High Court by Miss Sparrow. Miss Sparrow was diagnosed by her doctor to be suffering from a muscle virus. The doctor prescribed the use of Zendion Plus, one of the drugs manufactured by Kurall plc. He prescribed no other drugs to Miss Sparrow and explained to her that in no circumstances was she to take Zendion Plus in conjunction with any other medication. Miss Sparrow alleges that, far from curing her condition, Zendion Plus has made it worse. A medical report, prepared at the request of Kurall plc in contemplation of the litigation, concludes that 'it is almost certain that Miss Sparrow, at the time when she was taking Zendion Plus, was also taking other drugs, the nature of which, however, cannot be stated with accuracy'. Kurall plc wants to know how it may discover the nature of the other drugs used. Which one of the following courses of action would it be most appropriate to take?

[**A**] To apply for an order for specific disclosure.
[**B**] To apply under the Supreme Court Act 1981, s 34(2) for an order for disclosure against a non-party to the proceedings.
[**C**] To serve a request for further information on Miss Sparrow.
[**D**] To rely upon the tactic of surprise by awaiting trial and then cross-examining Miss Sparrow about the other drugs used.

**36.** During the trial of a claim commenced by Roger against William, the trial judge makes an order that a question be referred to the European Court of Justice. Which one of the following best describes the effect of such a reference?

**[A]** The English claim will be stayed until the European Court has given a preliminary ruling on the referred question, and the English courts will be bound by that ruling on that question.

**[B]** The English trial will immediately proceed, and the trial judge will decide all issues apart from the question referred to the European Court. The claim will then be adjourned until the European Court has given a ruling on the question, when judgment will be given by the English court.

**[C]** Roger and William will be required to agree the facts, which will be annexed to the reference to the European Court in a schedule, and the European Court will then give judgment to Roger or William in accordance with its decision on the question referred.

**[D]** The English claim will be discontinued, and Roger will be required to commence a fresh claim before the European Court, which will decide all the issues between the parties and give judgment accordingly.

**37.** Kate, who is making a claim for personal injuries, has made an application for an interim payment. The application was argued by counsel for both parties, and resulted in an interim payment of £4,000. The order made by the district judge says nothing about costs. What does this mean?

**[A]** That the costs of the application are included in the general costs of the claim and will be dealt with when the claim is finally determined.

**[B]** That payment of the costs of the application will be deferred until after the final determination of the claim.

**[C]** That no costs are payable between the parties in respect of the application.

**[D]** That because Kate won the application she is entitled to her costs of the application from the defendant.

**38.** Which one of the following propositions concerning notices to admit facts is INCORRECT?

[**A**] An admission made by a party in compliance with a notice to admit is made for the purposes of that claim only.
[**B**] An admission made by a party in compliance with a notice to admit may be withdrawn with the permission of the court.
[**C**] An admission made by a party in compliance with a notice to admit may not be used in favour of any person other than the person by whom the notice was given.
[**D**] If a party fails to reply to a notice to admit facts he will be deemed to admit the facts stated in the notice.

**39.** You have been briefed to attend a case management conference on behalf of the defendant in a contractual dispute. At the hearing the judge indicates a view of what he considers to be the only issues that ought to be tried, the issues identified by the judge being narrower than the issues raised by the parties' respective statements of case. Your opponent objects that the judge does not have power to narrow the issues in this way, and further indicates that he does not have instructions that will allow him to agree to the issues being narrowed in the way suggested by the judge. Which one of the following best describes the way the judge is most likely to deal with this situation in accordance with the rules?

[**A**] He should agree with your opponent, and leave the issues as they are.
[**B**] He is likely to adjourn the hearing to give your opponent an opportunity to get instructions on narrowing the issues.
[**C**] He is likely to adjourn the hearing to give your opponent an opportunity to get instructions, and is likely to make an order for the costs of the present hearing in favour of the defendant.
[**D**] He is likely to adjourn the hearing to give your opponent an opportunity to get instructions, coupled with a wasted costs order.

**40.** Fast Ltd have commenced a single claim against Slow Ltd claiming damages for breach of contract in respect of allegedly defective building work and also for damages for late completion of the building works. Slow Ltd have paid £15,000 into court 'in satisfaction of all the causes of action in respect of which the claimant claims'. In these circumstances, which one of the following propositions is CORRECT?

**[A]** When a payment into court is made where more than one cause of action is alleged, the defendant must allocate specific sums to each cause of action, so Slow Ltd's payment was irregular.

**[B]** Although Slow Ltd were entitled to make the Part 36 payment in the form they used, they can be asked to clarify how much of the payment relates to each cause of action, and the court may order them to clarify their payment notice.

**[C]** Slow Ltd had a choice as to whether to make the Part 36 payment in the form they used or by specifying individual sums for each cause of action, and Fast Ltd are not entitled to object to the form chosen.

**[D]** A payment into court must be in satisfaction of all the causes of action alleged in the proceedings, so Slow Ltd's payment was in the correct form.

**41.** You have been briefed on behalf of Helen, who is the respondent to an application issued by Terry five months before trial seeking an adjournment of the trial date. After a 30-minute hearing, the circuit judge granted the adjournment, and ordered Terry to pay Helen's costs of the application. How should Helen's costs be quantified?

**[A]** The circuit judge should immediately make a summary assessment of Helen's costs of the application.

**[B]** The circuit judge should adjourn the application to allow Helen's solicitors an opportunity to adduce evidence of the amount of costs incurred on Helen's behalf on the application.

**[C]** Helen's costs of the application will be assessed as part of the general costs of the claim once the claim is finally disposed of.

**[D]** Helen's costs of the application will be the subject of a detailed assessment by a district judge once Helen's solicitors have served a detailed bill of the costs relating to the application.

**42.** Thelma commenced proceedings in the county court against Darren, which were allocated to the fast track. One of the directions made in the claim required Thelma to serve a list of documents by 4 pm on Monday 20 November 2006. Darren's solicitors, who had been writing to Thelma's solicitors about the claim, included a fax number on their firm's printed letters. Thelma's solicitors had never asked Darren's solicitors for their consent to service by fax. At 6 pm on Friday 17 November 2006 Thelma's solicitors sent Thelma's list of documents to Darren's solicitors by fax. Which one of the following propositions is CORRECT?

[**A**] Service was defective because Thelma's solicitors have not obtained express written consent from Darren's solicitors for service by fax.
[**B**] Service was effective and took effect on Friday 17 November 2006.
[**C**] Service was effective and took effect on Saturday 18 November 2006.
[**D**] Service was effective and took effect on Monday 20 November 2006.

**43.** You have been briefed on behalf of the claimant in the trial of a claim that has been allocated to the fast track. Your first witness will be the claimant, Angela. Which one of the following best describes the form of your examination-in-chief?

[**A**] You must attempt to elicit the details relevant to the issues by asking Angela non-leading questions.
[**B**] You must attempt to elicit the details relevant to the issues by asking Angela, so far as possible, only leading questions.
[**C**] You must ask Angela to adopt her exchanged witness statement, and then elicit any further details by asking her non-leading questions.
[**D**] You must ask Angela to adopt her exchanged witness statement, and then elicit any further details by asking her leading questions.

**44.** In July 2000, Duff Aluminium Co Ltd ('Duff') delivered 30 tons of aluminium components to Peterborough Motor Manufacturing Plc ('Peterborough'). Peterborough paid Duff's invoice, but subsequently alleged that the components were too soft and useless. There has been voluminous correspondence between the parties, and solicitors have been instructed by both sides. Duff say that the soft aluminium identified by Peterborough must have come from another supplier. In May 2006 Peterborough's solicitors informed Duff's solicitors that a protective claim form had been issued in April 2006. In a letter sent in June 2006, marked 'without prejudice', Duff s solicitors replied:

> 'While it is denied that the soft aluminium came from our client, our client accepts there is a prospect of a court finding that in fact it did. We are at present seeking authority from our client as to proposals for settling this dispute, and would be grateful if you would consider postponing service for the time being so as to avoid unnecessary costs being incurred.'

It is now December 2006. The claim form has not been served, and the parties have been unable to agree terms despite a number of offers and counter-offers. Which one of the following is the best advice to give to Peterborough?

**[A]** Simply serving the expired claim form and hoping Duff will not take the point that it is no longer valid is not an option, because the limitation period has expired.

**[B]** Although on the facts there may be a good reason for not having served the claim form in time, any application to extend its period of validity will fail because there has been no attempt to serve it and its period of validity has expired.

**[C]** As it is marked 'without prejudice', the letter sent in June 2006 could not be referred to on any application to renew the claim form. Therefore Peterborough could only point to continuing negotiations, so any application to extend the validity of the claim form would fail.

**[D]** On the facts there is a good reason for not having served the claim form in time, so an application to extend its period of validity should succeed.

**45.** William was employed by Domestic Chemicals plc. In April 2001 there was an escape of chemical vapours at the plant where William worked. In January 2002 William attended a routine medical examination, after which he was informed that as a result of the April accident, he had suffered latent damage to his lungs which would fully develop in about two years. In March 2004 William developed symptoms of bronchial asthma and had to retire. In October 2005 he sought advice from a solicitor, who told him that he had a good cause of action against Domestic Chemicals. Proceedings were issued and served in November 2006. You would advise Domestic Chemicals that the date when the limitation period started to run was:

[**A**] April 2001.
[**B**] January 2002.
[**C**] March 2004.
[**D**] October 2005.

**46.** Sally, who is in business buying and selling motor cars, has applied for summary judgment for the sum of £4,000, being the price of a motor car sold to Brian. In his evidence in reply to the application Brian sets out a long list of defects in the car and says he is refusing to pay on the ground that the car was not of satisfactory quality. Exhibited estimates put the cost of curing the defects at £2,500. If Sally does not contest the facts set out in Brian's evidence, which one of the following orders is the district judge most likely to make?

[**A**] Dismissal of the application.
[**B**] A conditional order.
[**C**] Judgment for Sally in the sum of £1,500, dismissal of the application as to the balance.
[**D**] Judgment for Sally in the sum of £4,000 subject to a stay of execution in respect of £2,500.

**47.** April Fashions Ltd have served proceedings on Haymarket Insurance Plc claiming insurance monies alleged to be due under a policy after their premises were destroyed by fire. Haymarket have refused payment because they allege the fire was deliberately started by April Fashions' managing director. April Fashions' bank has foreclosed against the site of their former premises. Apart from the unpaid insurance monies April Fashions are clearly insolvent. On Haymarket's application for security for costs the Master considers that both sides have prospects of success at trial, but Haymarket's case is marginally stronger than that of April Fashions. How is the Master likely to deal with the application?

**[A]** He should disregard the merits of the case as they are not sufficiently overwhelming, and refuse the order because the defendants' refusal to pay on the policy contributed to April Fashions' financial problems, and to order them to provide security might stifle a genuine claim.

**[B]** Grant the order although April Fashions have an arguable claim, because the defendants are more likely to win at trial than April Fashions and April Fashions are clearly insolvent.

**[C]** Although he must always disregard the merits of the case, he should grant the order because April Fashions are clearly insolvent.

**[D]** Although he must take into account his finding that the defendants are more likely to win at trial than April Fashions, on balance he should refuse the order because the defendants' refusal to pay on the policy had contributed to April Fashions' financial problems and to order them to provide security might stifle a genuine claim.

**48.** You act for Laura, who is funding her case privately, and who is the claimant in a claim against Martin, who is covered by a certificate granting full representation under the Community Legal Service. At trial the county court judge decides all issues in favour of Laura. What should you say to the judge on the question of costs?

**[A]** That in the circumstances Martin should be ordered to pay Laura's costs of the claim, subject to determination of his liability to pay under the Costs Protection Rules.

**[B]** That as Martin is protected on costs because he is a publicly funded party, there should be no order as to costs.

**[C]** That as all issues have been decided in favour of Laura, Martin should be ordered to pay Laura's costs of the claim.

**[D]** That in the circumstances the question as to costs should be adjourned to allow the Legal Services Commission to intervene as you intend to apply for an order that the Legal Services Commission should pay Laura's costs of the claim.

**49.** Which one of the following propositions concerning service and execution of search orders is CORRECT?

**[A]** Execution of a search order must be supervised by a senior partner of the claimant's solicitors, who must be a person with experience of the operation of these orders.

**[B]** As a condition of the grant of a search order the claimant undertakes to the court that the order will only be executed in the presence of the defendant's solicitors.

**[C]** The defendant must be informed of his or her right to obtain legal advice before complying with the search order.

**[D]** Provided a supervising solicitor is present, there are no restrictions on who attends on behalf of the claimant when a search order is executed.

**50.** John sues Christopher for damage caused to his car during a three-car collision with cars driven by Christopher and Mary. Christopher wishes to claim against Mary for the damage done to his own car and wishes to claim a contribution from Mary in case he is held liable to John. Christopher is unsure how he should make these claims against Mary. Which one of the following is the CORRECT advice?

**[A]** He should issue an additional claim under Part 20 against Mary.
**[B]** He must issue separate proceedings against Mary.
**[C]** He only needs to write to Mary to inform her of the claims he has against her and the judge will do the rest at trial.
**[D]** He should serve a counterclaim against Mary.

## CIVIL EVIDENCE

**51.** As a general rule, answers given by a witness under cross-examination to questions concerning collateral matters must be treated as final. Which of the following is NOT one of the exceptions to the rule?

**[A]** Where the witness denies bias towards the party on whose behalf the cross-examination is being conducted.
**[B]** Where the testimony of the witness is unfavourable to the case of the party calling him or her.
**[C]** Where the witness denies that he or she has any previous convictions.
**[D]** Where the witness denies that he or she suffers from some physical or mental disability that affects the reliability of his or her evidence.

**52.** Larry, a landlord, has made a claim against Teresa. He alleges that contrary to the terms of the lease, for three months (March, April and May) Teresa, his tenant, has failed to pay the rent and has not cleaned her windows at monthly intervals. In her defence, Teresa denies these allegations, claiming that (i) she paid the rent for March, (ii) she cleaned the windows in March, and (iii) at the end of March, she and Larry, by agreement, brought the tenancy to an end.

Who bears the legal burden on the following three facts in issue:

(1) non-payment of rent;
(2) failure to clean the windows; and
(3) termination of the tenancy by agreement?

**[A]** Larry bears the legal burden on (1); Teresa on both (2) and (3).
**[B]** Larry bears the legal burden on both (1) and (2); Teresa on (3).
**[C]** Larry bears the legal burden on (2); Teresa on both (1) and (3).
**[D]** Teresa bears the legal burden on (1), (2) and (3).

**53.** Marcus was injured during the course of his employment with 5-X Brewery Ltd when the rung of a ladder on which he was required to stand when loading crates of lager collapsed, causing him to fall to the floor and damage his back. In his claim for damages against his employers he alleged, inter alia, that his place of work was not kept safe. Section 29(1) of the Factories Act 1961 states 'every place at which any person has at any time to work ... shall, so far as is reasonably practicable, be made and kept safe for any person working therein'. Who bears the evidential and legal burdens on the issue of whether it was 'reasonably practicable'?

**[A]** Marcus bears the evidential and legal burden.
**[B]** Marcus bears the legal burden; 5-X bear the evidential burden.
**[C]** 5-X bear the evidential and legal burdens.
**[D]** 5-X bear the legal burden; Marcus bears the evidential burden.

**54.** Printers Inc, a publisher, make a claim against another publisher, M & N Ltd, for infringement of copyright. M & N Ltd admit that there are strong similarities between passages in one of their recent publications, *Dieting Daily*, and passages in a book, *Daily Diets*, in which Printers Inc own the copyright, but allege that these similarities are purely coincidental. At the trial, Printers Inc wish to adduce evidence of three other books published by M & N Ltd that bear strong similarities to books in which other publishing houses own the copyright. Should the trial judge admit or exclude the evidence?

**[A]** Exclude the evidence, because Printers Inc have not alleged fraud or dishonesty.
**[B]** Exclude the evidence, because it is insufficiently relevant to the facts in issue.
**[C]** Admit the evidence, because it is relevant to the issue of whether the similarities between *Dieting Daily* and *Daily Diets* are merely coincidental or are due to copying.
**[D]** Admit the evidence, because it is relevant to show that M & N Ltd have a disposition to commit conduct of the kind alleged.

**55.** Which of the following propositions concerning the law of evidence in CIVIL proceedings is INCORRECT?

**[A]** Questions relating to the law of any jurisdiction other than England and Wales are issues of fact to be decided, on the evidence given with respect to that law, by the judge.
**[B]** At common law a judge has no discretionary power to exclude evidence that is relevant and admissible as a matter of law solely on the ground that it may have been unlawfully obtained.
**[C]** Evidence of the character of a party or a witness is admissible only if it is among the facts in issue.
**[D]** The appropriate standard of proof in proceedings for committal to prison arising out of a civil contempt of court is proof beyond reasonable doubt.

**56.** John is suing ABC Ltd, claiming damages for breach of warranty, or alternatively for fraud. John took delivery of a boiler for his new restaurant. On the night he first opened the restaurant to the public, the boiler blew up and his specially invited guests were unable to dine. John alleges that one of the directors of ABC Ltd had represented to him that the boiler had been specially reconditioned and was as good as new, and that there was clearly a fraudulent misrepresentation because the director knew the boiler had not been reconditioned. What standard of proof is appropriate at the trial?

**[A]** On a balance of probabilities for breach of warranty and fraud.
**[B]** Beyond reasonable doubt for breach of warranty and fraud.
**[C]** On a balance of probabilities for the breach of warranty but beyond reasonable doubt for the fraud.
**[D]** Beyond reasonable doubt for the breach of warranty but on a balance of probabilities for the fraud.

**57.** Which of the following propositions is INCORRECT?

**[A]** A child may give unsworn evidence in civil proceedings.
**[B]** A spouse of a party to civil proceedings is competent to testify for that party.
**[C]** A spouse of a party to civil proceedings is not competent to testify against that party.
**[D]** It is possible for a competent and compellable witness in civil proceedings to refuse to answer specific questions on the grounds of privilege.

**58.** Which of the following presumptions is NOT capable of putting either a legal or evidential burden on the party against whom it operates?

**[A]** The presumption of legitimacy.
**[B]** The presumption of continuance of life.
**[C]** The presumption of formal validity of a marriage.
**[D]** The presumption of death.

**59.** Consider the following types of statement.

(i) A previous inconsistent statement made by a person called as a witness and proved, by virtue of s 4 or s 5 of the Criminal Procedure Act 1865, in cross-examination.
(ii) A previous statement made by a person called as a witness and proved for the purpose of rebutting a suggestion that that witness's evidence has been recently fabricated.
(iii) A statement in a document, made by a person called as a witness and used to refresh that witness's memory, which, by reason of cross-examination on the document, is made evidence in the proceedings.

In CIVIL proceedings, which of these statements is admissible as evidence of any fact stated therein?

**[A]** The statements in (i) and (ii) but not (iii).
**[B]** The statements in (ii) and (iii) but not (i).
**[C]** The statements in (i) and (iii) but not (ii).
**[D]** The statements in (i), (ii) and (iii).

**60.** Charlie entered into a loan agreement with Smart Finance Ltd. The loan was repayable by monthly instalments. Some months into the agreement, Charlie fell into financial difficulties and stopped making repayments. Proceedings were brought by Smart Finance Ltd for the recovery of the outstanding debt. Barry has sole responsibility for processing each instalment repayment received by Smart Finance Ltd. Each payment is then forwarded to a member of the secretarial staff who enters the amount and the name of the sender onto a spreadsheet. At the end of each day, the spreadsheet is checked by Barry for its accuracy. At trial, Barry gives evidence for Smart Finance Ltd. In his evidence-in-chief, he is asked whether a particular repayment had been received but has no recollection of whether or not it had been. May he refresh his memory from the spreadsheet before continuing to give his evidence?

**[A]** Yes, but only if the spreadsheet was checked by Barry while the details of the payment were still fresh in his memory.
**[B]** No, because Barry has no independent recollection of the payment having been received.
**[C]** No, because the entry in the spreadsheet would be hearsay evidence.
**[D]** No, because the entry in the spreadsheet was not made by Barry.

**61.** Philip is suing his employer for damages for negligence and breach of statutory duty arising out of an accident at work in which he was injured while operating a press. The employer is alleging contributory negligence. Immediately after the accident, Quentin, a fellow worker and witness to the accident, went to the foreman, Robert, and said that Philip had failed to follow the correct safety procedures before operating the press. Robert went to his supervisor, Sylvia, and told her what Quentin had said. Sylvia then went to the Safety Officer, Tariq, and told him what Quentin had said.

The employer wishes to rely on Quentin's oral statement for the truth of its contents. Assuming compliance with any relevant procedural requirements, which of the following best describes the manner in which that statement may be proved?

**[A]** By the evidence of Quentin (in which case, the statement shall not be given in evidence without the permission of the court).
**[B]** As in [A] or, if Quentin is not called, by the evidence of Robert.
**[C]** As in [A] or, if Quentin is not called, by the evidence of Robert or Sylvia.
**[D]** As in [A] or, if Quentin is not called, by the evidence of Robert, Sylvia or Tariq.

**62.** Beneficiaries make a claim against their trustee in the Chancery Division, alleging misuse of trust funds. The trustee is cross-examined as to the spending of the trust monies for his own purposes. He declines to answer, because his answer would incriminate him of the offence of theft.

Which of the following CORRECTLY describes the evidential position?

**[A]** He must not answer.
**[B]** He can refuse to answer and, if he does, cannot be liable for contempt of court.
**[C]** He must answer, but his answer cannot be used against him in the civil proceedings.
**[D]** He must answer, but his answer cannot be used against him should he subsequently be prosecuted for theft.

**63.** David, a pedestrian, is called on behalf of Euan at the trial of a negligence claim made by Euan to recover the cost of repairs to his car, which was involved in a collision with another car. David testifies that he saw both cars travelling at about 30 mph, that the defendant's vehicle was no more than five yards behind Euan's car, and that the defendant failed to stop in time when Euan had to brake suddenly at a zebra crossing. Although he has been a passenger in cars many times, David has never held a driver's licence. Is David's evidence admissible or inadmissible?

**[A]** Inadmissible because he is not qualified as an expert.
**[B]** Admissible non-expert opinion evidence.
**[C]** Inadmissible evidence of fact, ie evidence containing no statements of opinion.
**[D]** Inadmissible because it relates, in part, to the ultimate issues in the case.

**64.** In the course of a contractual dispute between Dick and Wei-Ming, Dick sent Wei-Ming a letter marked 'Private and Confidential' in which he disputed liability but offered Wei-Ming 50% of the amount he was claiming as due to him. Wei-Ming declined this offer and is now suing. Dick in his defence denies any liability. Wei-Ming would like to put Dick's letter in evidence. Is it admissible?

**[A]** Yes, because it was not marked 'without prejudice'.
**[B]** No, because it has no relevance to Dick's liability.
**[C]** No, because it should be treated as if written without prejudice.
**[D]** No, because its prejudice is greater than its probative value.

**65.** Raymond is suing Steve for damages for injuries that Raymond suffered when their cars collided at a crossroads. Raymond alleges that Steve was negligent. Raymond will rely on the fact that Steve has been convicted by the local Magistrates' Court of driving carelessly at the time of their collision. Steve will deny negligence and claim that the conviction was erroneous.

On the issue of Steve's negligence, which one of the following statements best describes the legal position?

**[A]** Raymond must prove Steve's negligence.
**[B]** Raymond must prove Steve's negligence and will raise a rebuttable presumption of this by proving Steve's conviction.
**[C]** Whether Raymond proves Steve's conviction or not, Steve must prove he was not negligent.
**[D]** Raymond must prove Steve's negligence and will do so conclusively by proving Steve's conviction.

**66.** Jason, whilst receiving radiation treatment from some newly installed equipment in an NHS hospital, was given a serious overdose. When Jason indicated that he would sue the hospital authority, the authority contacted the equipment manufacturers, who asked the authority for a report from the technician in charge. The technician supplied a report to the authority. They sent one copy to the manufacturers and another to their solicitors. Jason, who is now suing the hospital authority, wants to inspect the report, but the authority are claiming privilege for it, saying that one of its purposes was to get legal advice in case they were sued. Are they entitled to withhold the report?

**[A]** No, if the main purpose of the report was to find out what went wrong and to prevent it in future.
**[B]** No, because it was from the technician to his employers and therefore not a solicitor–client communication.
**[C]** Yes, irrespective of its purpose.
**[D]** Yes, if ordered to do so by the Minister of Health.

**67.** Imran is suing Denise. At the disclosure stage, Denise's solicitor, Tom, inadvertently sent Imran's solicitor, Henry, a copy of a document for which legal professional privilege could properly have been claimed. When Tom realises his mistake and informs Denise, she makes a claim against Imran for delivery up of any copies of the document and for an injunction to restrain him from making any use of the information contained in them.

Which of the following best describes the approach of the court in determining her claim?

[**A**] The evidence will be admitted if sufficiently relevant to the issues in the case.

[**B**] The evidence will only be admitted if the interests of Denise in keeping the information confidential outweigh the interests of Imran in seeking to make use of it.

[**C**] The court should not generally allow such evidence to be used but may do so if it is in the public interest in the proper administration of justice to do so.

[**D**] The court should allow such evidence to be adduced unless a reasonable solicitor in the position of Henry would have realised that he had been permitted to see the document by reason of an obvious mistake.

**68.** In a civil claim made by Philip against Denise arising out of the collision of two ships, both of which sank, aerial photographs taken of the two ships after the collision but before they sank have been admitted in evidence. Wendy, an expert in the field of maritime accident reconstruction, gives evidence that she examined the aerial photographs and consulted two articles (of which she is not the author) in a technical journal called *Maritime Accident Reconstruction Monthly*. She also testifies that the journal is a source upon which maritime accident experts generally rely. Lastly she testifies that on the basis of her examination of the photographs, coupled with the information obtained from the articles, 'Denis's ship almost certainly crashed into the side of Philip's ship'. Assuming compliance with all relevant procedural requirements, was this evidence properly admitted?

**[A]** No, because it was evidence of opinion based in part on facts that were not within Wendy's personal knowledge.
**[B]** No, because it contained an opinion on the ultimate facts in issue in the case.
**[C]** No, because Wendy's evidence alone could not be used to establish that the journal is a source on which experts in this field generally rely.
**[D]** Yes.

**69.** A national newspaper suggests that a new bishop's appointment has been made on political grounds. The bishop sues for libel. At the trial, the journalist who wrote the article gives evidence that the bishop was appointed after making a large donation to the political party in power and after undertaking to support government policy when appointed. When asked to name the sources of his information the journalist refuses, saying that he has a privilege under the Contempt of Court Act 1981, s 10. How should the judge rule?

**[A]** He has an absolute right to refuse to disclose his source.
**[B]** He need not answer unless it is established that it is 'necessary' in the interests of justice or national security or for the prevention of disorder or crime.
**[C]** He must not answer without his source's consent because the public interest requires free access to the media to expose official wrongdoing.
**[D]** He must answer.

**70.** Cherie is suing Daniel for breach of contract. Cherie, in the light of a statement made by Edward to her (Cherie's) solicitors, calls Edward as a witness. Edward gives evidence that totally contradicts the statement, and the judge allows him to be treated as hostile.

Is the statement admissible?

[**A**] No, because hearsay.
[**B**] Yes, for the truth of its contents and to establish Edward's inconsistency.
[**C**] Yes, but *only* to establish Edward's inconsistency.
[**D**] No, because irrelevant.

# THE CRIMINAL MCT

# [TIME LIMIT: 3 HOURS]

## CRIMINAL LITIGATION AND SENTENCING

**1.** You represent Samantha who consents to summary trial on a charge of receiving stolen goods. You intend to call Samantha herself and a character witness. You can:

**[A]** make both an opening and a closing speech as of right.
**[B]** make an opening speech, and then apply to the magistrates to allow you to make a closing speech as well.
**[C]** make only a closing speech since the only witness whom you are calling other than the accused is not a witness of fact.
**[D]** make only a closing speech since in a summary trial the defence cannot make an opening speech.

**2.** Gerald is arrested in connection with the murder of Harriet. He has been informed of his rights. He has now been lawfully detained for a period of 96 hours. The investigation is not yet complete, and the police wish to detain him for further questioning. In these circumstances, the investigating officers must:

**[A]** take him before a Magistrates' Court who may authorise detention for a further 36 hours.
**[B]** obtain authorisation from an officer of not less than the rank of superintendent, who may authorise detention for a further six hours.
**[C]** release him or charge him.
**[D]** release him on bail and then immediately re-arrest him for the murder of Harriet.

**3.** Here are four separate situations involving Mike (aged 15). In the first three, he appears in court with Neville (aged 18). Only summary offences are involved. Mike and Neville always plead not guilty.

In which one of the following situations does the adult Magistrates' Court have NO discretion to send Mike to the Youth Court for trial?

**[A]** Neville appears in the Magistrates' Court with Mike. Mike is charged with driving whilst disqualified; Neville is charged with aiding and abetting him.

**[B]** Mike and Neville appear in the Magistrates' Court jointly charged with taking a car without the owner's consent.

**[C]** Mike and Neville appear in the Magistrates' Court on two separate charges. Neville is charged with common assault against Peter, and Mike is charged with common assault against Robert, the two assaults allegedly occurring during a brawl involving all four people.

**[D]** Mike appears alone in the Magistrates' Court to be tried on a charge of assaulting a police officer in the execution of his duty. The magistrates start the trial under the mistaken impression that Mike is 18 years old but then discover his true age.

**4.** Tom appeared in the Magistrates' Court charged with theft. He was released on bail, the sole condition being that he surrender to custody at Ashbridge Magistrates' Court in seven days' time.

The day before Tom was due to return to the Magistrates' Court, a police officer saw him at Ashbridge railway station. Tom was about to board a train and had a large suitcase in his hand. The officer, believing that Tom was going away and was unlikely to surrender to the court on the due date, arrested Tom.

Tom wants advice on whether the arrest at the railway station was lawful or not. Which one of the following statements is CORRECT?

**[A]** The police officer had no power to arrest Tom. He should have applied immediately to a magistrate for a warrant to arrest Tom.

**[B]** The police officer had no power to arrest Tom. He should have waited to see if Tom attended court on the due date. If Tom had failed to attend court, a bench warrant for his arrest could then have been sought.

**[C]** The police officer had the power to arrest Tom provided that his belief that Tom would not surrender to custody at the court was a reasonable belief.

**[D]** The police officer had the power to arrest Tom because Tom had been charged with theft, which is an arrestable offence.

**5.** Daniel and Edward both appear in the Magistrates' Court. Daniel is charged with theft of a television set and Edward is charged with dishonestly receiving the television set, knowing or believing it to be stolen. They do not wish to be tried together. Your advice to them should be that:

**[A]** as both offences arise out of the same incident, they will be tried together automatically.
**[B]** they cannot be tried together unless they both agree.
**[C]** as this is not a joint charge, there will automatically be separate trials.
**[D]** they will be tried together if the magistrates decide that the offences are so related to each other that a joint trial is necessary in the interests of justice.

**6.** Frank is charged with criminal damage and burglary. The facts alleged by the prosecution are that Frank broke a window, valued at £75 (the criminal damage) to gain access to property from which he stole various specified items (the burglary). In these circumstances:

**[A]** Frank may elect trial on indictment for the burglary, but the criminal damage must be tried summarily.
**[B]** Frank may elect trial on indictment for both offences.
**[C]** Frank has no right to elect trial on indictment.
**[D]** Frank may elect trial on indictment for the burglary, and the criminal damage may be included, by the prosecution, in the indictment.

**7.** Frank is sent to Barchester Crown Court to stand trial on a charge of burglary. He fails to attend court on the date fixed for his trial. He is charged with the offence of failing without reasonable cause to surrender to custody, under the Bail Act 1976, s 6. Which one of the following statements about the Bail Act offence is CORRECT?

**[A]** The offence should be dealt with at the Crown Court by a judge sitting alone.
**[B]** The offence should be dealt with at the Crown Court by a judge sitting with a jury.
**[C]** The offence should be dealt with at the Crown Court by a judge sitting with two magistrates.
**[D]** The offence is a purely summary one and so must be dealt with by the Magistrates' Court.

**8.** Alan was charged with assault occasioning actual bodily harm. He was not legally represented. When the charge was put to him in the Magistrates' Court, he said: 'Guilty but I was acting in my own defence.' After hearing mitigation the magistrates proceeded to sentence him. Alan subsequently seeks advice on appeal. You should advise him that:

**[A]** he can appeal against conviction to the Crown Court, which may quash the conviction and substitute an acquittal if it decides that the plea was equivocal.
**[B]** he can appeal against sentence only as he pleaded guilty.
**[C]** he can appeal against conviction to the Crown Court and that appeal will take the form of a retrial.
**[D]** he can appeal against conviction to the Crown Court on the basis that the plea was equivocal and, if the Crown Court decides that the plea was equivocal, it will remit the case to the magistrates to rehear on a not guilty plea.

**9.** Julie (aged 16) and Alf (aged 19) are jointly charged with theft. They appear together in the Magistrates' Court and both plead guilty. Which one of the following statements regarding the sentencing of Julie is CORRECT?

**[A]** The Magistrates' Court must sentence Julie.
**[B]** The Magistrates' Court must remit Julie to the Youth Court for sentence.
**[C]** The Magistrates' Court may sentence Julie if its powers of sentence are appropriate; otherwise, it will remit her to the Youth Court for sentence.
**[D]** The Magistrates' Court may commit Julie to the Crown Court for sentence.

**10.** Francesca (aged 22) pleads guilty to theft at the Greenbridge Magistrates' Court. Being of the opinion that the offence is so serious that greater punishment should be inflicted for the offence than they have power to impose, the Greenbridge magistrates commit her for sentence under s 3 of the Powers of Criminal Courts (Sentencing) Act 2000, to the Pencaster Crown Court. The Pencaster Crown Court imposes a sentence of three months' imprisonment. Francesca now wishes to appeal to the Court of Appeal against that sentence.

Which one of the following statements is CORRECT?

**[A]** Francesca may appeal to the Court of Appeal as of right.
**[B]** Francesca may appeal to the Court of Appeal only if the Crown Court judge certifies that the case is fit for appeal.
**[C]** Francesca cannot appeal to the Court of Appeal.
**[D]** Francesca may appeal to the Court of Appeal with the leave of a single judge of the Court of Appeal.

**11.** Nicky is aged 14. He appears in the Youth Court, charged alone with several burglaries of dwelling houses (such burglary being punishable with up to 14 years' imprisonment following conviction on indictment in the case of an adult offender). The value of property stolen in the burglaries is over £20,000. The Youth Court decides to send Nicky to the Crown Court for trial.

Which one of the following statements is CORRECT?

**[A]** He can be sent for trial because a Crown Court judge might lawfully pass a sentence under s 91 of the Powers of Criminal Courts (Sentencing) Act 2000.
**[B]** He must be sent for trial because the Youth Court has no jurisdiction to try a case where the offence carries a sentence of 14 years' imprisonment or more.
**[C]** He cannot be sent for trial because he is not charged together with an adult and a sentence under s 91 of the Powers of Criminal Courts (Sentencing) Act 2000 would not be lawful in his case.
**[D]** He cannot be sent for trial because juveniles cannot be tried in the Crown Court for burglary of a dwelling.

**12.** James fails to attend his summary trial for an offence of theft by shoplifting. At his last appearance before the court on that charge, he consented to summary trial and he was told of the time and date of his trial. The magistrates:

**[A]** must adjourn the case until James is present.
**[B]** have a discretion to hear the case on the basis of a not guilty plea.
**[C]** must proceed to hear the case on the basis of a not guilty plea.
**[D]** must proceed to deal with the case and, as James has failed to appear, have a discretion as to whether to treat him as if he had pleaded guilty.

**13.** Jacob is arrested in connection with an offence of robbery. On Jacob's arrival at the Police Station, a decision to detain him is made at 8 am by Police Constable Brown, who is not involved in the investigation. Reviews of Jacob's detention are held by Sergeant Green at 2 pm and 11 pm. Jacob is given substantial meals at 12.30 pm and 6 pm and short breaks in the interrogation every two hours. He has now been in custody for 23 hours without charge, and consults a solicitor. What advice should his solicitor give him about his detention?

**[A]** The detention should have been reviewed at 2 pm, 8 pm and 2 am.
**[B]** The detention should have been reviewed at 2 pm, 8 pm and 2 am, and those reviews and the original decision to detain should have been carried out by officers of higher ranks.
**[C]** The times of the reviews are correct but those reviews, and the original decision to detain, should have been carried out by officers of higher ranks.
**[D]** He has no legitimate ground of complaint.

**14.** Mario is charged with possession of an offensive weapon in a public place. At his trial in the Magistrates' Court, he contends that the place where he was found in possession of the weapon was not a 'public place'. The magistrates decide that the place was, in law, a 'public place'. Mario is convicted. He wishes to appeal against his conviction. Which one of the following statements is INCORRECT?

**[A]** He may appeal against his conviction to the Crown Court, and the appeal will take the form of a rehearing.
**[B]** He may issue a claim form seeking the permission of the High Court to appeal by way of case stated.
**[C]** He may make an application to the magistrates asking them to state a case for the opinion of the High Court.
**[D]** If he appeals to the High Court by way of case stated, he loses his right to appeal to the Crown Court.

**15.** Harry is tried summarily on a charge of assault occasioning actual bodily harm. He is found guilty and fined. He wishes to appeal against conviction, but not against sentence. He asks you for advice as to any adverse implications for him. You should advise him that the Crown Court:

**[A]** can order him to pay the prosecution's costs but cannot increase the sentence.
**[B]** cannot order him to pay the prosecution's costs but can increase his sentence to the maximum that the magistrates could have imposed.
**[C]** can order him to pay the prosecution's costs and can increase the sentence to the maximum that the magistrates could have imposed.
**[D]** can order him to pay the prosecution's costs and can increase the sentence to the maximum that the Crown Court could have imposed if he had been tried on indictment.

**16.** When considering the seriousness of an offence for the purpose of sentencing, the court may, under the Criminal Justice Act 2003, treat certain circumstances as amounting to aggravating factors enabling it to increase the sentence. Which one of the following cases does NOT disclose an aggravating factor identified in the Act?

**[A]** An offence motivated by gender.
**[B]** An offence motivated by racial grounds.
**[C]** An offence motivated by sexual orientation.
**[D]** An offence motivated by disability.

**17.** Martha is charged with burglary. She initially admitted the offence when interviewed by the police, but now she says that she only confessed because she had been bullied by the police officers. She intends to plead not guilty and will say that, at the time of the burglary she was at a nightclub with a friend, Zoe. She intends to call Zoe as a defence witness. Which of the following does Martha have to disclose to the prosecution?

**[A]** Where she claims to have been at the time of the burglary.
**[B]** Zoe's name, address, and date of birth.
**[C]** The fact she is going to argue that her confession is inadmissible.
**[D]** All of the above.

**18.** Members of a jury are unable to reach a verdict and the judge discharges them. Which one of the following statements is CORRECT?

**[A]** There must be a retrial.
**[B]** There may be a retrial if the prosecution wish to proceed.
**[C]** The charge against the defendant is left on the file marked not to be proceeded with unless the Crown Court or the Court of Appeal gives leave.
**[D]** The defendant is acquitted.

**19.** Nickie, aged 21, appears at the Crown Court on a charge of burglary. The court has power to impose the following sentences except one. Which one?

**[A]** A custody plus order.
**[B]** An intermittent custody order.
**[C]** A suspended sentence.
**[D]** A suspended custody plus order.

**20.** Sheila was sent for trial on a charge of theft of a camera, this being the only charge before the magistrates. The papers sent to the Crown Court disclosed, among other things, that she was arrested the day after the alleged theft when she tried to sell the camera, for a fraction of its usual price, to a plain-clothes policeman. The indictment contains a single count alleging theft. At the end of the prosecution's evidence in the Crown Court, the prosecution seek leave to add a second count alleging handling stolen goods, namely the camera. This application:

**[A]** will succeed, unless, having regard to the merits of the case and the possibility of adjourning, the new count cannot be added without injustice to Sheila.

**[B]** will fail, because the counts in the indictment must correspond with the charges that were sent for trial.

**[C]** will fail, because all applications relating to the form of the indictment must be made on arraignment, and it is now too late.

**[D]** is unnecessary because the prosecution have an absolute right to amend the form of an indictment at any time.

**21.** Darren pleads guilty in the Magistrates' Court to theft. He now tells you that the offence was in fact committed by Eric, who bullied him into taking the blame for it, saying that Darren's little boy 'would live to regret it' if he did not. Darren now wishes to appeal to the Crown Court. In this situation:

**[A]** he has no right to appeal against conviction, but may do so with the leave of the Crown Court, and, if leave is given, the case will be reheard in the Crown Court.

**[B]** he has no right to appeal against conviction but may challenge the validity of the plea, and, if that challenge is successful, the case will be remitted to the magistrates for rehearing.

**[C]** he has no right to appeal against conviction, but may do so with the leave of the Magistrates' Court, and if leave is given, the case will be reheard in the Crown Court.

**[D]** he has the right to appeal against conviction by serving notice on the Magistrates' Court and the magistrates will rehear the case themselves.

**22.** An indictment contains a single count for robbery. The judge in her summing up directs the jury that they may find the defendant 'not guilty of robbery but guilty of theft', and the jury bring in such a verdict. Their verdict is:

**[A]** valid, because robbery includes by implication an allegation of an offence of theft.
**[B]** valid, because theft is a less serious offence than robbery.
**[C]** invalid, because sufficient particulars for a count alleging theft cannot be arrived at by deleting particulars from the existing robbery count.
**[D]** invalid, because the jury is only empowered to return a verdict in respect of those offences for which the accused has been arraigned.

**23.** Toby is charged with racially aggravated assault. At the plea and case management hearing, he tells you that he would plead guilty if he could be sure that he would not receive a custodial sentence. He asks whether you can find out what sort of sentence the judge will pass. Which one of the following statements is INCORRECT?

**[A]** The judge should give an indication of sentence only if requested by the defendant.
**[B]** The judge is not obliged to give an indication of sentence and may refuse to do so without giving reasons.
**[C]** Where there is uncertainty about the factual basis of the plea, as where the defendant and the prosecution put forward different versions of what occurred, the judge, if giving an indication, should give an indication for each scenario.
**[D]** An indication is binding on the judge and on any other judges who become involved in the case.

**24.** Rupert, aged 16, appears in the Youth Court and is found guilty of four offences of sexual assault. The offences are triable either way and the maximum sentence for each offence is ten years. Which one of the following statements about the justices' powers is CORRECT?

When sentencing, the justices may:

**[A]** impose a detention and training order for a total of no more than 24 months.
**[B]** impose a detention and training order for a total of no more than 12 months.
**[C]** commit him to the Crown Court for sentence where he may be sentenced to a maximum custodial sentence of 12 months per offence to run consecutively, amounting to four years in aggregate.
**[D]** commit him to the Crown Court for sentence where he may be sentenced to a maximum custodial sentence of ten years per offence to run concurrently, amounting to ten years in aggregate.

**25.** At the end of the prosecution case, counsel for the defence makes a submission of no case to answer. The judge rejects this submission and orders the trial to continue. The alleged defect in the prosecution case is rectified by cross-examination of the defence witnesses. The defendant is convicted, and appeals solely on the basis that the judge was wrong to reject the submission.

Assuming that the judge was wrong in law to reject the submission, which of the following actions is the Court of Appeal most likely to take?

**[A]** Quash the conviction, because, had the judge not erred, the defendant would have been acquitted.
**[B]** Quash the conviction, and order a *venire de novo*.
**[C]** Uphold the conviction if satisfied that the judge directed the jury properly when he summed up.
**[D]** Examine the evidence given during both the prosecution and defence cases, and decide the appeal on that basis.

**26.** John is charged with indecent assault upon Tracey. It is alleged that the assault took place in one of the cubicles at the physiotherapy department of the hospital where John works as a porter. The only prosecution evidence is that of Tracey and her mother (who says that Tracey returned home in a distressed state on the day in question). After the jury have retired, they send a note to the judge asking for further evidence, namely whether or not the adjacent cubicles were in use at the time of the alleged assault so that any protests by Tracey might have been heard. As counsel in the case, you are asked by the judge whether he can comply with this request. What should you say to him?

**[A]** The jury are only entitled to hear additional evidence if the judge first gives leave to the prosecution to re-open their case.
**[B]** The jury are entitled to ask for any additional evidence provided that the evidence is given in open court, in the presence of the accused and of both counsel.
**[C]** The jury are not entitled to ask any questions once they have retired.
**[D]** The jury are not entitled to hear additional evidence after they have retired.

**27.** Stan has been remanded in custody by the Magistrates' Court following a fully argued bail application. He wishes to challenge the refusal of bail. Which one of the following statements is CORRECT?

**[A]** He may apply for bail to the Crown Court or to the High Court.
**[B]** He may apply for bail to the Crown Court and, if the Crown Court refuses bail, he may apply to the High Court.
**[C]** He may apply for bail to the Crown Court.
**[D]** His only option is to make a further application to the Magistrates' Court, showing a material change in circumstances since the last application to that court.

**28.** Bill, aged 18, appears at the Magistrates' Court and is convicted of one charge of aggravated motor vehicle taking. He has three previous findings of guilt for taking motor vehicles without consent. What is the maximum custodial sentence which may be imposed by the magistrates?

**[A]** Twelve months.
**[B]** Sixty-five weeks.
**[C]** Two years.
**[D]** Ten years.

**29.** Daniel is charged with burglary (contrary to s 9(1)(b) of the Theft Act 1968) at Pencaster Crown Court, in that he entered a building as a trespasser and stole a television set. The evidence, from both the prosecution and the defence, shows that he had had permission both to enter the building and to borrow the television set, but that he had failed to return it when he should because he had decided to keep it permanently. Daniel is convicted and now appeals to the Court of Appeal. The Court of Appeal accepts that he did not enter as a trespasser, and that he had permission to borrow the television set, but holds that he had wrongfully and dishonestly retained it and did not intend to return it to its owner. In these circumstances, which of the following courses of action is the Court of Appeal most likely to adopt?

**[A]** It will quash the conviction.
**[B]** It will uphold the conviction.
**[C]** It will quash the conviction, but substitute a conviction for theft.
**[D]** It will quash the conviction and order a retrial.

**30.** Joseph is charged with assault occasioning actual bodily harm and is to be tried in the Magistrates' Court. Which of the following statements is correct with regard to any material held by the prosecution?

**[A]** The prosecution must disclose any unused material that might undermine their case.
**[B]** The prosecution must disclose any unused material that might assist Joseph's case.
**[C]** As disclosure in the Magistrates' Court is voluntary, the prosecution do not have to disclose any unused material.
**[D]** The prosecution must disclose any unused material that might undermine their case or assist Joseph's case.

**31.** If a jury that has been given a majority verdict direction is still unable to reach a verdict, the judge may give it further directions. According to the decisions of the Court of Appeal these further directions must NOT include one of the following elements. Which one?

**[A]** That the jurors have a duty to act not only as individuals but also collectively.
**[B]** That jurors should be willing to give and take.
**[C]** That jurors should be prepared to alter their views if they can do so and still remain consistent to the oath that they have taken.
**[D]** That jurors should bear in mind the cost and inconvenience of a fresh trial if they cannot reach a verdict.

**32.** Alan was sent to the Crown Court for trial on a charge of burglary. The papers sent to the Crown Court when the case was transferred there also indicated that Alan had perpetrated an offence of theft (which was wholly unconnected with the alleged burglary); however Alan was not sent for trial on any charge of theft. The prosecution preferred two indictments – one containing the count of burglary, the other a count of theft. At the trial of the burglary indictment Alan was acquitted. At the trial of the theft indictment an application by Alan's counsel to have the indictment quashed was rejected by the trial judge.

The trial judge's decision was:

**[A]** incorrect because the prosecution can never prefer an indictment that charges an offence which was not sent for trial.
**[B]** incorrect because the prosecution can only prefer an indictment that charges an offence which was not sent for trial if the offence in question could properly be joined (in the same indictment) with the offences that were sent for trial.
**[C]** correct because the prosecution can always prefer an indictment in respect of any offence that is disclosed by the papers sent to the Crown Court (whether or not that charge has been sent for trial).
**[D]** correct because the prosecution can prefer an indictment in respect of any offence that falls within the same statute as an offence for which an accused has been sent for trial.

**33.** Peter, aged 27, appeared before the Magistrates' Court and pleaded guilty to a charge of assault occasioning actual bodily harm arising out of an incident that had occurred at a public house. The maximum penalty for that offence is five years. The court considers that a community sentence is warranted. Which of the following orders is NOT within the court's powers?

[**A**] An attendance centre requirement.
[**B**] A curfew requirement.
[**C**] An exclusion requirement.
[**D**] An alcohol treatment requirement.

**34.** Susie appears at the Crown Court charged with handling stolen goods. The prosecution allege that the goods were worth £20,000. Susie pleads guilty to the charge but, in her mitigation, contends that the goods were in fact worth only £5,000. The judge hears no evidence on the value of the goods. When passing sentence, he states that he is sentencing Susie on the basis that the goods were worth £20,000. Susie wishes to appeal against sentence. Which one of the following statements most accurately reflects the advice that you should give to Susie?

[**A**] The Court of Appeal is likely to replace the sentence with the sentence appropriate to the handling of goods worth £5,000.
[**B**] The Court of Appeal is likely to remit the case to the Crown Court with a direction that the judge should hear evidence on the value of the goods.
[**C**] The Court of Appeal is likely to hear evidence on the value of the goods itself.
[**D**] She has no ground for appeal.

**35.** Arnold, aged 20, is sentenced to two years' imprisonment by a Crown Court judge. He wishes to appeal against this sentence. In these circumstances, which one of the following statements is CORRECT?

**[A]** Arnold does not need leave to appeal, because the sentence is wrong in law.

**[B]** Arnold can only get leave from the single judge of the Court of Appeal, because the appeal is against sentence.

**[C]** Arnold can appeal only if he obtains the leave of the trial judge.

**[D]** Arnold may either get leave to appeal from the single judge of the Court of Appeal, or a certificate from the trial judge that the case is fit for appeal.

**36.** Gareth, a Welsh nationalist, is charged with the murder of Harry, an English motorist. The prosecution case is that Gareth, while standing on a bridge over a busy road, rolled a granite boulder over the edge and onto the road, and that the boulder fell through the windscreen of Harry's car, causing him multiple injuries from which he died within minutes. Gareth gives evidence admitting these facts but denying that he intended to cause death or serious bodily harm to Harry. Which of the following would be the best way in which to direct the jury on the question whether they may infer that Gareth intended death or serious bodily harm as a result of his actions?

**[A]** 'You should decide whether Gareth intended death or serious bodily harm by reference to all the evidence, drawing such inferences as appear proper in the circumstances.'
**[B]** 'You are not entitled to infer that Gareth intended death or serious bodily harm as a result of his actions.'
**[C]** 'If you are satisfied that death or serious bodily harm was a natural and probable consequence of Gareth's actions, then you should infer that he intended death or serious bodily harm as a result of those actions.'
**[D]** 'You may only infer that Gareth intended death or serious bodily harm as a result of his actions if he has failed to satisfy you that he did not intend death or serious bodily harm.'

**37.** Jane is charged on indictment with obtaining property by deception from Harrods, having ordered goods on a credit account using a false name. At the trial, counsel for Jane, on her behalf, admits that she had opened this account. May the prosecution rely on counsel's admission?

**[A]** No, because the admission was not in writing.
**[B]** Yes, because the admission was made orally in court.
**[C]** No, because counsel's admission can never bind Jane.
**[D]** Yes, because although the admission is inadmissible, the judge will exercise his discretion to admit it.

**38.** Fred and Harry are jointly charged with blackmailing their employer. Fred pleads not guilty; Harry pleads guilty. The prosecution wish to call Fred's wife, Ghisha, and Harry's wife, Irene, to give evidence. Are Ghisha and Irene competent and compellable to give evidence for the prosecution?

**[A]** Ghisha is competent and compellable; Irene is competent but not compellable.
**[B]** Ghisha is competent but not compellable; Irene is competent and compellable.
**[C]** Both Ghisha and Irene are competent but not compellable.
**[D]** Both Ghisha and Irene are competent and compellable.

**39.** Phil is charged with the attempted rape of Tina shortly after a party at a nightclub. The prosecution allege that Tina was in an alleyway, just after the nightclub had closed, where she was approached by Phil, who tried to rape her. When she screamed, he ran off. Phil maintains that he honestly believed that Tina was willing to have sexual intercourse and, as soon as he realised she was not, he left. At trial, Phil wishes to adduce evidence of a conversation with a friend whom he met as he was leaving the nightclub and who told him that he had just had sexual intercourse with a girl in the alleyway and she was 'up for it'. Phil also wishes to cross-examine Tina about her behaviour at the nightclub, where she had taken part in a competition exposing her breasts. Prosecution counsel does not object to the admission of the evidence of the conversation but intends to object to Phil's application to cross-examine Tina about her behaviour at the nightclub even though counsel concedes that the evidence is relevant to Phil's defence. On what basis is counsel most likely to do so?

**[A]** Questions about the previous sexual behaviour of the complainant in proceedings for sexual offences are not permissible.
**[B]** The prejudicial effect of the evidence would outweigh its probative value.
**[C]** Tina's behaviour at the nightclub did not take place at or about the same time as the event that is the subject matter of the charge.
**[D]** Refusing Phil leave to cross-examine Tina would not render unsafe any conclusion of the court and/or the jury.

**40.** Michael is charged with sexually assaulting Nora. The case for the prosecution is that he and Nora were sitting together in a train travelling from London to Oxford and that shortly after the train passed through Reading, Michael put out his hand and touched Nora's breasts. Michael admits that he and Nora were sitting together in the train, but denies that he touched her. When the police (lawfully) searched Michael's briefcase they discovered a number of pornographic magazines containing pictures of naked women. On what basis is the prosecution most likely to seek to admit the evidence of the pornographic magazines?

**[A]** The evidence is important explanatory evidence.
**[B]** The evidence rebuts Michael's denial of the offence.
**[C]** The evidence is relevant to an important matter in issue between the defendant and the prosecution.
**[D]** The evidence corrects a false impression of innocence given by the defendant's plea of not guilty.

**41.** Carlos is charged with murder and raises the defence of self-defence. Which party bears the evidential and legal burdens in relation to the defence raised and what standard of proof is required to discharge the legal burden?

**[A]** The evidential burden is on the defence; the legal burden is on the prosecution and will be discharged by proof beyond reasonable doubt.
**[B]** The evidential burden is on the defence; the legal burden is also on the defence and will be discharged by raising a reasonable doubt.
**[C]** The evidential burden is on the defence; the legal burden is also on the defence and will be discharged by proof on a balance of probabilities.
**[D]** The evidential burden is on the prosecution; the legal burden is on the defence and will be discharged by proof beyond reasonable doubt.

**42.** Patrick, who is French, is charged with the theft of a packet of batteries from a shop in High Holborn. It is alleged that he entered the shop, took the batteries from a shelf, put them into his pocket, rushed out of the shop, and ran away. At his trial (in London), he gives evidence through an interpreter. Cross-examined about his knowledge of English, he denies that he can speak English. The prosecution now wish to introduce evidence to show that Patrick is fluent in English. Should they be allowed to do so?

[**A**] Yes, because the jury is entitled to know that Patrick was prepared to lie on oath.
[**B**] Yes, because such evidence is likely to lead the jury to reappraise Patrick's evidence on the facts in issue in the case.
[**C**] No, because of the rule of finality of answers to questions concerning collateral matters.
[**D**] There is no clear answer, because the cases show that the difference between questions going to credit and questions going to the issue has been reduced to vanishing point.

**43.** Tom, who has previous convictions for offences of dishonesty, is charged with burglary. He does not give evidence but his counsel, having been granted leave by the court under s 100 of the Criminal Justice Act 2003, puts to the chief witness for the prosecution that he (the witness) has two previous convictions for theft, as in fact is the case. The witness denies that he has such convictions. On these facts, consider the following propositions:

(i) Counsel for the prosecution may make a formal admission that the witness has the two convictions for theft.
(ii) Counsel for the defence may prove the fact of the convictions for theft.
(iii) Evidence of Tom's convictions cannot be admitted because Tom does not give evidence.

Which of these propositions is INCORRECT?

[**A**] (i) only.
[**B**] (i) and (ii), but not (iii).
[**C**] (ii) and (iii), but not (i).
[**D**] (iii) only.

**44.** Naseem is charged with murder. Shortly after the incident, he told Malcolm, a friend, that his defence would be one of self-defence. At the trial, Naseem gives evidence of self-defence. Consider the following two statements:

(i) Naseem's words to Malcolm are prima facie inadmissible as a previous consistent statement.
(ii) Naseem's words to Malcolm are admissible if the prosecution put it to Naseem that he has invented the defence only after hearing the prosecution case to serve his own purposes at the trial.

Which of the above statements is CORRECT?

[**A**] Only (i).
[**B**] Only (ii).
[**C**] Neither.
[**D**] Both.

**45.** Which of the following statements best describes the position at trial where a witness has previously identified the accused out of court, an identification which the defence alleges to be mistaken?

[**A**] Evidence of the out-of-court identification is inadmissible.
[**B**] Evidence of the out-of-court identification is admissible, but only after the witness has identified the accused in court.
[**C**] Evidence of the out-of-court identification is admissible, but only if the witness has been unable to identify the accused in court.
[**D**] Evidence of the out-of-court identification is admissible and this should be elicited prior to the witness identifying the accused in court.

**46.** Alf is charged with the murder of a woman cyclist by deliberately driving his car at her. The prosecution can prove that in the week before the alleged murder, in separate incidents Alf had driven his car at two other women cyclists, knocking them off their bicycles. Alf's defence is accident. Could evidence of the other incidents be admissible?

**[A]** No, evidence of a propensity to commit offences of the kind charged is not admissible.
**[B]** No, because it is irrelevant.
**[C]** Yes, because evidence of a propensity to commit offences of the kind charged may be admissible if admitting such evidence would not have an adverse effect on the fairness of the proceedings.
**[D]** Yes, because evidence of a propensity to commit offences of the kind charged is always admissible.

**47.** Simon is charged with robbery. The prosecution case is that he robbed Jenny of her handbag and its contents while she was walking home from work late one night. Immediately after the robbery had taken place, Jenny called the police. She told them that she would be able to recognise her attacker. The officers drove her around the local area during which time she saw Simon standing outside a nearby takeaway restaurant and positively identified him as the robber. Simon was arrested and taken to the police station. In interview he denies any involvement in the offence and requests an identification procedure. It would be practicable for the police to hold one. Which one of the following statements is CORRECT?

**[A]** The police must hold an identification procedure because Simon disputes being the person Jenny claims to have seen.
**[B]** The police must hold an identification procedure because Simon has requested one.
**[C]** The police must hold an identification procedure unless it would serve no useful purpose in proving or disproving whether Simon was involved in committing the offence.
**[D]** The police are not permitted to hold an identification procedure when a positive street identification has been made.

**48.** Sonam is charged with dangerous driving. The prosecution case is that while Charles was crossing a road using a pelican crossing (a pedestrian crossing controlled by traffic lights) he was struck by a motor car being driven by Sonam. At trial, during his examination-in-chief Charles says that the traffic lights were showing green for pedestrians and red for traffic when he started to cross the road. However, in his witness statement made three days after the incident Charles had stated that he could not be sure whether the traffic lights were showing green for pedestrians or not. In cross-examination by Sonam's counsel, Charles accepts that he made the earlier statement. However, he maintains that the traffic lights were showing green for pedestrians and red for traffic. Which one of the following statements concerning the evidential status of Charles' previous statement is CORRECT?

**[A]** It is inadmissible because it is hearsay.
**[B]** It is only evidence of Charles' inconsistency.
**[C]** It is evidence of (i) Charles' inconsistency and/or (ii) the status of the traffic lights.
**[D]** It does not form part of the evidence in the case because the statement was contained in Charles' witness statement and was not given during in his evidence-in-chief.

**49.** Morgan is charged with sexually assaulting a nine-year-old girl in the town park at 4 pm on 11 September last year. His defence is mistaken identity. In evidence he states that he has 'never been in trouble with the police before'. In fact he has a previous conviction for indecent exposure. What would be the best justification for admitting evidence of that previous conviction?

**[A]** The previous conviction shows he is dishonest and not to be believed on oath.
**[B]** He has attacked the character of a prosecution witness.
**[C]** It is evidence to correct a false impression given by Morgan.
**[D]** The previous conviction shows a general propensity towards offences of a sexual nature.

**50.** The following statements concern evidence of the character of the accused. Only one is CORRECT. Which one?

**[A]** At common law, evidence of the accused's bad character may be admitted if it relates to offences that are strikingly similar to those with which the accused is charged.
**[B]** Where an accused elects not to testify but relies on wholly exculpatory statements made to the police, and evidence of the good character of the accused is properly admitted in evidence, the judge should direct the jury on the relevance of this evidence in relation to the guilt of the accused.
**[C]** The word 'character' as used in the Criminal Justice Act 2003 refers only to general reputation.
**[D]** The word 'character' as used in the Criminal Justice Act 2003 refers only to specific offences committed in the past.

**51.** James is charged with burglary. The items stolen in the burglary were recovered from a trunk in Clinton's garage. Clinton says that James brought the trunk to his home on the night of the burglary and asked if he could store it in Clinton's garage for two weeks while he was moving house. James claims that he does not know Clinton and did not leave a trunk at his garage. At trial, Clinton is called as a prosecution witness. James wishes to cross-examine Clinton regarding his two previous convictions for burglary. The prosecution do not agree to the admission of this evidence.

In these circumstances, consider the following statements:

(i) Clinton's previous convictions will be admissible, in principle, if they have substantial probative value in relation to a matter in issue in the proceedings that is of substantial importance in the context of the case as a whole;
(ii) Clinton's previous convictions will be admissible, in principle, at common law because they are relevant to Clinton's credibility;
(iii) leave of the court must be given before evidence of Clinton's bad character can be given.

Which of these statements, if any, is accurate?

**[A]** (i), but not (ii) or (iii).
**[B]** (i) and (iii), but not (ii).
**[C]** (i) and (ii), but not (iii).
**[D]** All of them.

**52.** Amanda is charged with blackmail. Police officers claim that when they called at Amanda's house on a totally unrelated matter (routine door-to-door enquiries about a missing child), Amanda, on seeing them, had said: 'It's about the blackmail isn't it? I'm sorry. I knew you'd catch me sooner or later.' Amanda admits that the officers called and asked about a missing child, but categorically denies that she ever made the alleged confession: she alleges that the officers have invented the confession (but does not allege any other improper behaviour on their part). The prosecution intend to call the police officers to prove Amanda's confession. Is such evidence admissible?

**[A]** Yes, but only if the judge holds a voir dire and gives a ruling to this effect.
**[B]** No, because Amanda categorically denies making the confession.
**[C]** Yes, and without recourse to a voir dire.
**[D]** No, because hearsay.

**53.** Sam is charged with murdering his wife, Tina, by stabbing her with a knife. The prosecution case is that the reason for the offence was the discovery by Sam that Tina was having an adulterous affair with his best friend, Victor. According to Sam, however, he made no such discovery. The day before the alleged murder, Tina wrote a letter to Vera, a friend, stating: 'Yesterday, Sam discovered me and Victor in bed together!' Are the contents of this letter admissible?

**[A]** No, because they are hearsay.
**[B]** Yes, in principle, under the Criminal Justice Act 2003, s 117.
**[C]** Yes, as part of the *res gestae*.
**[D]** Yes, in principle, under the Criminal Justice Act 2003.

**54.** Cos is charged with conspiring to utter forged banknotes. At his trial it emerges that his involvement in the offence came about as the result of an approach made to him by an undercover police officer, who said that he had a number of associates interested in buying counterfeit currency. Cos was then introduced to further undercover police officers posing as ready and willing purchasers of forged notes. The judge is of the view:

(i) that the evidence of the undercover police officers has been obtained by improper and unfair means;
(ii) that the prejudicial effect of the evidence of the undercover police officers does NOT outweigh its probative value.

In principle, what power, if any, does the judge have to exclude the evidence?

[**A**] The judge may only exclude the evidence under s 78 of PACE 1984.
[**B**] The judge may only exclude the evidence under the common law discretion.
[**C**] The judge may exclude the evidence under s 78 of PACE 1984 or under the common law discretion.
[**D**] The judge has no power to exclude the evidence.

**55.** Anthony is charged with theft. Shortly after his arrest his girlfriend. Beatrice, visits him at the police station, where he makes a full confession to her about his involvement in the theft. At trial Beatrice gives evidence that Anthony confessed after she had told him that he would get bail if he did so. Anthony's counsel submits that the confession should be excluded under the Police and Criminal Evidence Act 1984, s 76(2)(b) (likelihood of unreliability). The trial judge finds that Beatrice probably did make the statement about bail but nevertheless rules that the confession is admissible. This ruling could have been CORRECT on only one of the following grounds. Which one?

[**A**] Under s 76, a confession is always admissible if obtained by someone other than a person in authority.
[**B**] The judge was satisfied that Anthony's confession was true.
[**C**] The judge was satisfied that Anthony's confession was not obtained in consequence of Beatrice's statement.
[**D**] There is an overriding discretion to ignore the effect of s 76(2)(b) and include confession statements.

**56.** Michael, aged 20, is tried on indictment for sexual assault. The prosecution case depends substantially on a confession he made to two police officers who interviewed him after his arrest. No other person was present at the interview. The trial judge, on a voir dire relating to the admissibility of this confession, concludes that Michael is 'mentally handicapped' (as defined in the Police and Criminal Evidence Act 1984). Which of the following statements about this case is CORRECT?

**[A]** The judge, having concluded that Michael is mentally handicapped, is required by law to exclude Michael's confession.
**[B]** If the judge admits Michael's confession, he is required by law to warn the jury that there is a special need for caution before convicting the accused in reliance on the confession.
**[C]** Having regard to his mental handicap, Michael will necessarily be incompetent to give evidence.
**[D]** Michael may give sworn evidence, but only if he satisfies the judge that he understands the divine sanction of the oath.

**57.** Omar and Rupert have been convicted of an armed bank robbery. Photographs taken by a security camera automatically at five-second intervals during the course of the raid were produced at the trial. No identification witnesses were called, but the jury were invited to look at the photographs, look at the defendants in the dock and conclude, if they thought it right to do so, that the men in the photographs were in fact the men in the dock. Omar and Rupert appeal on the ground that the photographs were improperly admitted. Is the appeal likely to succeed?

**[A]** Yes, because admission of the photographs was in breach of the hearsay rule.
**[B]** No, because the photographs were admissible under the Criminal Justice Act 2003, s 117.
**[C]** Yes, because the admission of the photographs was in breach of the rule against previous consistent statements.
**[D]** No, because photographs are in a class of their own to which neither the rule against hearsay nor the rule against previous consistent statements applies.

**58.** Rob is charged with murdering Onye. Tom, an associate of Rob, says, on his death-bed, that he, not Rob, murdered Onye. Tom dies before Rob's trial. Subject to any discretion that the judge may have to exclude it, Tom's statement is admissible. On what basis?

**[A]** Under the Police and Criminal Evidence Act 1984, s 76 as a confession.
**[B]** Under the Criminal Justice Act 2003, s 116.
**[C]** As part of the *res gestae.*
**[D]** Under the Criminal Justice Act 2003, s 117.

**59.** Robin is charged with handling a stolen video recorder. His defence is that he purchased it, without knowledge or belief that it was stolen, from a former neighbour who has since emigrated. At his trial, Robin's barrister admits on his behalf that the recorder was stolen. He claims that the neighbour had said to him at the time of the purchase: 'I bought it from a shop last Christmas, though I haven't kept the receipt or guarantee.' At trial, evidence of what the neighbour allegedly said to him will be admissible, for the defence. On what basis?

**[A]** As part of the *res gestae.*
**[B]** As evidence of Robin's lack of knowledge or belief that the goods were stolen.
**[C]** As evidence that the goods were not stolen.
**[D]** Under s 116 of the Criminal Justice Act 2003.

**60.** Whenever a trial judge directs the jury on the proper use of lies by the accused to support evidence of guilt, the direction should make it clear to the jury that they should be satisfied on all the following matters except one. Which one?

**[A]** That the lie was deliberate.
**[B]** That the lie was in writing or otherwise recorded in documentary form.
**[C]** That there was no innocent motive for the lie.
**[D]** That the lie relates to a material issue.

**61.** Joan is charged with theft. At her trial she challenges under the Police and Criminal Evidence Act 1984, s 76(2)(b) (likelihood of unreliability) the admissibility of a confession she made to the police. The judge rules that the confession is admissible holding that:

(i) s 76(2)(b) requires some element of improper conduct on the part of the interrogator (which is absent in Joan's case);
(ii) the test is whether the confession Joan made was obtained in consequence of anything said or done that was likely, in the circumstances existing at the time, to render unreliable any such confession that might be made by her in consequence thereof.

Is the judge's ruling on these points CORRECT or INCORRECT?

**[A]** Correct on the first point; incorrect on the second.
**[B]** Correct on both points.
**[C]** Incorrect on the first point; correct on the second.
**[D]** Incorrect on both points.

**62.** Piero is suspected of committing a series of burglaries. The police arrested him and detained him for questioning. He made a full confession and was charged with the burglaries. At his trial, he challenges the admissibility of the confession, representing that it was obtained by oppression. The trial judge makes two rulings:

(i) that he will only hold a voir dire if the defence adduce some evidence in support of their representation;
(ii) that if such a voir dire does take place, he will be entitled to enquire into the truth of the confession. Is the judge's ruling on these points CORRECT or INCORRECT?

**[A]** Incorrect on both points.
**[B]** Correct on both points.
**[C]** Incorrect on the first point; correct on the second.
**[D]** Correct on the first point; incorrect on the second.

**63.** Jim was overtaken by a yellow Ford Escort car and made a mental note of the registration number, V937 NWX. Moments later the Escort pulled out to overtake on the brow of a hill and an oncoming car driven by Ken was forced to swerve off the road and into a ditch. Jim stopped and told a police officer, Luke, what he had seen, including the registration number of the Ford Escort. The Ford Escort is traced to Adam who is charged with dangerous driving. Jim cannot be found despite the police making every effort to trace him. Can the prosecution call Luke to prove the registration number of the Ford Escort by giving evidence of what Jim told him?

[**A**] No, because it is hearsay.
[**B**] Yes, in principle, under the Criminal Justice Act 2003, s 116.
[**C**] Yes, in principle, under the Criminal Justice Act 2003, s 117.
[**D**] Yes, as original evidence.

**64.** Brian is charged with burglary. It is alleged that he broke into Warne's Warehouse and stole a large quantity of electronic goods. The police find a piece of paper inside the warehouse on which is written, 'Brian is cool'. The piece of paper is found near to a jemmy that was used to break into the warehouse. Traces of ink are found on the jemmy that match the ink used on the piece of paper. The prosecution wish to adduce the piece of paper as evidence that Brian was in the warehouse. Is the piece of paper admissible?

[**A**] Yes, as real evidence.
[**B**] No, because it is hearsay.
[**C**] Yes, in principle, under the Criminal Justice Act 2003, s 116.
[**D**] Yes, in principle, under the Criminal Justice Act 2003, s 117.

**65.** François is charged with theft. The case against him depends substantially on the correctness of a visual identification of him by Clare, which François alleges to be mistaken. At the trial, the judge comes to the conclusion that the quality of Clare's identification evidence is poor. What should he do?

**[A]** Leave the case to the jury, but with the proviso that in his summing up he must give an adequate warning to the jury about the special need for caution before convicting François in reliance on the correctness of the identification.
**[B]** Direct an acquittal, whatever the nature of the other evidence in the case.
**[C]** Direct an acquittal, unless there is other evidence that goes to support the correctness of the identification evidence.
**[D]** As in [C], but subject to the proviso that if there is supportive evidence, he must direct the jury that if he had thought there was insufficient identification evidence, he would have directed them to acquit.

**66.** Dave is charged with arson and conspiracy to defraud an insurance company following a fire at a factory owned by ABC Electronics, a company of which he is the managing director. Tegid, a police officer, attended the scene shortly after the fire had started. As a man resembling Dave cycled past, Tegid heard a woman shout: 'Dave! I can't believe you are cycling away when your factory is on fire.' The prosecution now wish to call Tegid to give evidence of what the woman shouted in order to prove that Dave was the arsonist. Which one of the following statements is CORRECT?

**[A]** Tegid's evidence will not be hearsay because he can give first-hand evidence of what the woman said.
**[B]** Tegid's evidence will be hearsay if the purpose of the woman in making the statement was to cause another person to believe that the cyclist was Dave.
**[C]** Tegid's evidence will be hearsay irrespective of the purpose of the woman in making the statement.
**[D]** Tegid's evidence will only be hearsay if the purpose of the woman in making the statement was to cause Tegid to act on the basis that the cyclist was Dave.

**67.** Adam is standing trial for the murder of his wife. He will adduce evidence in support of his defence of provocation. At the trial the prosecution call a police officer who gives evidence that Adam consulted his solicitor and then, on being questioned under caution about his suspected involvement in the offence, remained completely silent. The defence accept that at that stage Adam failed to mention the facts he will rely on in support of his defence and also that they are facts that, in the circumstances existing at the time, Adam could reasonably have been expected to mention.

In these circumstances, consider the following statements:

(i) The court, in deciding whether there is a case to answer, may draw such inferences from Adam's failure to mention the facts as appear proper.
(ii) The court or jury, in deciding whether Adam is guilty of the offence charged, may draw such inferences from Adam's failure to mention the facts as appear proper.
(iii) Adam cannot be convicted of murder solely on an inference drawn from his failure to mention the facts.

Which of these statements, if any, is accurate?

[**A**] None of them.
[**B**] (i) and (ii), but not (iii).
[**C**] (ii) and (iii), but not (i).
[**D**] All of them.

**68.** Michael is charged with assaulting Paul, a fellow employee. In his defence, Michael claims that he was acting in reasonable self-defence (although Michael accepts that Paul had only lightly tapped him on the arm). Michael says in evidence that his mother died shortly before the alleged assault and he was feeling particularly sensitive at the time. He wishes to call a psychiatrist to give evidence that shortly after the alleged offence he, Michael, appeared to be a person suffering from severe sorrow following a recent bereavement, that he was likely to overreact to any adverse circumstances, but was not suffering from any mental illness. Will the psychiatrist's evidence be admissible?

**[A]** Yes, because it is the evidence of a qualified medical practitioner in his field of competence and is relevant to Michael's defence.
**[B]** Yes, but only in order to confirm the credibility of Michael's testimony as to his state of mind.
**[C]** No, because it is a self-serving statement in that the psychiatrist is simply repeating what Michael told him after the event.
**[D]** No, because the tribunal of fact does not need expert assistance in assessing Michael's alleged mental condition at the relevant time.

**69.** Marie was suspected by Naomi, a store detective, of shoplifting. She was detained and questioned about her suspected commission of the offence by Naomi and (according to Naomi) eventually admitted that she was shoplifting. At Marie's trial her counsel wishes to argue that her confession should be excluded under the Police and Criminal Evidence Act 1984, s 78 because Naomi had interviewed Marie without complying with the Code of Practice for interviews made pursuant to s 66 of that Act (Code C). Would such an argument be justified?

**[A]** No, because Naomi's questioning of Marie could not have been an interview for the purposes of Code C.
**[B]** Yes, because on the facts the judge *could* conclude that Naomi was bound to comply with Code C.
**[C]** No, because only the police are bound to comply with Code C.
**[D]** Yes, because anyone who questions a suspect must comply with Code C.

**70.** George is charged with attempted burglary. At his trial a constable gives evidence that on his arrival at the scene of the crime, industrial premises surrounded by barbed-wire fencing, George was running away, that on arresting him he noticed that George's clothing was badly torn in several places, that he reasonably believed that the tears in George's clothing might have been the result of George's commission of the offence, that he told George of his belief and asked him to account for the condition of his clothing, and that George had replied: 'I don't have to, and I won't!'

On these facts, may the court, in deciding whether there is a case to answer, draw such inferences as appear proper from George's refusal to account for the condition of his clothing?

**[A]** Yes.
**[B]** No, because such inferences can be drawn only from failure or refusal to account for the presence of objects on the person or in or on a person's clothing.
**[C]** No, because George was not told by the constable, when asking him to account for the condition of his clothing, the effect of failing or refusing to do so.
**[D]** No, because it is only in deciding whether George is guilty that the court may draw inferences from his refusal to account for the condition of his clothing.

# APPENDIX 1

# ANSWERS TO THE CIVIL MCT

**CIVIL LITIGATION**

| | | | |
|---|---|---|---|
| 1. | C | 26. | D |
| 2. | D | 27. | C |
| 3. | B | 28. | D |
| 4. | C | 29. | D |
| 5. | D | 30. | B |
| 6. | A | 31. | A |
| 7. | B | 32. | B |
| 8. | C | 33. | C |
| 9. | B | 34. | D |
| 10. | D | 35. | C |
| 11. | B | 36. | A |
| 12. | A | 37. | C |
| 13. | D | 38. | D |
| 14. | B | 39. | D |
| 15. | A | 40. | B |
| 16. | A | 41. | A |
| 17. | D | 42. | D |
| 18. | C | 43. | C |
| 19. | C | 44. | B |
| 20. | D | 45. | B |
| 21. | B | 46. | C |
| 22. | A | 47. | A |
| 23. | C | 48. | A |
| 24. | B | 49. | C |
| 25. | A | 50. | A |

**CIVIL EVIDENCE**

| | | | |
|---|---|---|---|
| 51. | B | 61. | D |
| 52. | B | 62. | D |
| 53. | C | 63. | B |
| 54. | C | 64. | C |
| 55. | C | 65. | B |
| 56. | A | 66. | A |
| 57. | C | 67. | C |
| 58. | B | 68. | D |
| 59. | D | 69. | B |
| 60. | A | 70. | B |

# APPENDIX 2

# ANSWERS TO THE CRIMINAL MCT

**CRIMINAL LITIGATION AND SENTENCING**

| | | | |
|---|---|---|---|
| 1. | B | 21. | B |
| 2. | C | 22. | A |
| 3. | B | 23. | C |
| 4. | C | 24. | A |
| 5. | D | 25. | A |
| 6. | D | 26. | D |
| 7. | A | 27. | C |
| 8. | D | 28. | A |
| 9. | C | 29. | C |
| 10. | D | 30. | D |
| 11. | A | 31. | D |
| 12. | B | 32. | B |
| 13. | C | 33. | A |
| 14. | B | 34. | A |
| 15. | C | 35. | D |
| 16. | A | | |
| 17. | D | | |
| 18. | B | | |
| 19. | D | | |
| 20. | A | | |

**CRIMINAL EVIDENCE**

| | | | |
|---|---|---|---|
| 36. | A | 51. | B |
| 37. | B | 52. | C |
| 38. | B | 53. | D |
| 39. | D | 54. | A |
| 40. | C | 55. | C |
| 41. | A | 56. | B |
| 42. | C | 57. | D |
| 43. | D | 58. | B |
| 44. | D | 59. | B |
| 45. | D | 60. | B |
| 46. | C | 61. | C |
| 47. | C | 62. | A |
| 48. | C | 63. | B |
| 49. | C | 64. | A |
| 50. | B | 65. | C |
| | | 66. | B |
| | | 67. | D |
| | | 68. | D |
| | | 69. | B |
| | | 70. | C |

# APPENDIX 3

# NOTE-FORM ANSWERS TO THE CIVIL MCT

## CIVIL LITIGATION

The reader may be concerned as to whether the questions in this book are of the same length as those appearing in the MCTs set for the Bar Vocational Course. The average length of the questions in the Civil Litigation section for one of the MCT tests set for the students on the Bar Vocational Course was 166 words per question. In that test, the shortest question had 65 words, and the longest had 311 words. Obviously this varies from year to year depending on which questions are used. However, conscious efforts are made to ensure that long questions are balanced by the use of short questions as well. Question 1 in this book is 118 words long, question 2 has 167 words, question 3 has 111 words, and question 4 has 175 words. In the Civil MCT in this book, the shortest question is number 16 with 82 words, and the longest is question 44 which has 357 words.

**1.** The first one or two questions in the Civil Litigation MCT are intended to be relatively straightforward. When this question has appeared in the tests it has presented few problems. In order to answer this question it is necessary to have learnt the basic conditions that must be established before the court will consider granting a search (previously an *Anton Piller*) order. These were laid down by Ormrod LJ in *Anton Piller KG v Manufacturing Processes Ltd* [1976] Ch 55, and can be found in the **Civil Litigation Manual** at **16.3**. The question asks you to identify the incorrect condition, which is answer [C]. This answer is, to some extent, disguised by the fact that search orders are in practice most commonly applied for in intellectual property cases, but there is no formal condition restricting the making of these orders to such cases. Some people are prone to make unnecessary mistakes when faced with questions asking for the INCORRECT answer, so perhaps extra care should be taken when answering this form of question.

**2.** Under the Civil Procedure Rules (CPR), rr 10.3 and 15.4(1), the defendant's obligation (in non-specialist proceedings) to file a defence or acknowledgment of service arises after service of the particulars of claim (and not the claim form unless it is indorsed with or served with the particulars of claim). In the question particulars of claim have not been served, so the defendant is not in default and consequently the claimant cannot enter a default judgment at this stage (r 12.3). The correct answer is therefore [D]. Answer [B] has its attractions as Part 8 claims are outside the scope of judgment in default (CPR r 12.2). However, a claim for specific performance of a contract will almost certainly raise a substantial dispute of fact, so the Part 8 procedure is inappropriate (see CPR r 8.1(2)).

**3.** This is a personal injuries claim, so the High Court would be used only if the total award is likely to exceed £50,000 (CPR PD 7, para 2.2). The £50,000 threshold is the global sum excluding interest, costs and benefits recoupment, and also ignoring any contributory negligence (High Court and County Courts Jurisdiction Order 1991). On the facts, minor bruising is unlikely to exceed perhaps £400, so the total award of approximately £2,600 makes this an inappropriate case for the High Court (answers [A] and [C]). As to track allocation, CPR r 26.6(1) provides that for personal injuries cases the small claims track is the normal track if the total award will not exceed £5,000 and if damages for pain, suffering and loss of amenity will not exceed £1,000. This claim is within both limits, so the normal track is the small claims track, answer [B].

**4.** This question concerns the interrelation between additional claims under Part 20 and the main proceedings between the claimant and the defendant. As shown by *Stott v West Yorkshire Road Car Co Ltd* [1972] 2 QB 651, discussed in the **Civil Litigation Manual** at **9.4.9**, in many ways proceedings under an additional claim have a life independent of the main claim. However, it is important to distinguish:

(a) additional claims seeking a contribution or indemnity; and
(b) additional claims for substantially similar remedies.

Contribution and indemnity claims brought by way of additional claims against persons not already parties in the case are obviously dependent on the outcome of the claim by the claimant against the defendant. If the claimant loses against the defendant, there is nothing for the third party to contribute towards and nothing to indemnify the defendant against. Therefore, if the claimant's action does not proceed to trial, such as where it is dismissed or struck out, and the additional claim raises only a contribution or an indemnity, there is no reason for the additional claim to proceed to trial, and it will fall with the claimant's action. However, additional claims in category (b) above go beyond reimbursing the defendant for any liability the defendant may have to the claimant, so will continue to trial (if need be) despite the claimant's action being, eg, struck out or dismissed. In the question Eric has the following additional claims against George: one in category (a) (the indemnity) and one in category (b) (the damages claim). Hence the correct answer is [C].

**5.** Marine Fish Ltd wish to bring proceedings against a defendant who is outside the jurisdiction. The proposed defendant is domiciled in France (for which see the **Civil Litigation Manual** at **11.2.4**). Service out of the jurisdiction on EC-domiciled defendants is governed by the Jurisdiction Regulation (Council Regulation (EC) No. 44/2001), see **11.2.1**. Proceedings should normally be commenced in France by virtue of Article 2 (see **11.2.3**). The fact the damage was suffered by Marine Fish Ltd in England gives it the alternative of suing in England by virtue of Article 5(3) (see **11.2.5.3**). If it chooses to sue in England, proceedings may be commenced without permission (see **11.2.2**). Hence the correct answer is [D]. Notice the use of the word 'must' in answers [A] and [B]. There is no need to seek permission under CPR, r 6.20 (see **11.3**), answer [C].

**6.** You need to be alert to the fact that this question asks for the INCORRECT answer. When parties have solicitors acting for them it is usually the solicitors who take all steps for them in the proceedings. A significant exception is the signing of disclosure statements. Although there are exceptions where insurers have interests in the litigation (see CPR, r 31.10(9) and PD 31, para 4.7), the general rule is that disclosure statements must be signed by the party rather than their solicitor, see r 31.10(6)). Rule 31.10(6) is an important rule and not a mere technicality (*Arrow Trading and Investments Est 1920 v Edwardian Group Ltd* [2005] 1 BCLC 696). Answer [A] should therefore have been selected.

Answer [B] makes the point that disclosure covers anything on which information is recorded (including videos and computer discs), and is not restricted to paper documents (see the **Civil Litigation Manual** at **20.4**). Answer [C] refers to the need to make a reasonable search (see **20.4.4**). Answer [D] refers to the practice of giving disclosure by serving a list of documents (in Form N265), and to the usual position that case management directions will include a timetable for doing so.

**7.** Gillian is defending a claim, and wishes to raise a human rights point as an answer to the claim. She must therefore set out the point giving precise details of the Convention right relied upon, the alleged infringement, and any relief sought in her statement of case (here the defence), see PD 16, para 15.1 and the **Civil Litigation Manual** at **5.3**. The correct answer is therefore [B]. This question is a great deal more difficult than it might appear, because the other answers all point to things that Gillian's legal representatives would be well advised to do in order to advance her case on the alleged infringement of her Convention rights. It may well be very advisable to seek a determination of the point as a preliminary issue (answer [A]), and her counsel will certainly need to deal with it in the trial skeleton argument (answer [C]) and during oral argument at trial (answer [D]). However, these answers do not address when the point should first be raised, which is the way this multiple choice question is formulated.

**8.** Siew Leng has made a claimant's Part 36 offer to the defendant, Martha (see the **Civil Litigation Manual** at **27.8**). Although these offers are made without prejudice save as to costs, this means they can be relied upon for the purposes of costs and related questions. Answer [A] is therefore incorrect. Answer [B] is incorrect because it is the fact Siew Leng has been awarded judgment for £90,000 that shows she has succeeded, not the fact she made a claimant's Part 36 offer. This answer does no more than state the general position when a claimant wins a case, and fails to address the real significance of making a realistic claimant's Part 36 offer. Answer [C], on the other hand, is correct because it summarises the discretion available to the court to award enhanced costs and interest orders where judgment exceeds the terms of a claimant's Part 36 offer, see CPR, r 36.21. Answer [D] correctly says that the offer can be taken into account on the question of costs, but incorrectly says this is likely to be exercised by granting Siew Leng her standard basis costs. That is the usual order in the absence of a claimant's Part 36 offer. The point behind making such an offer is to give grounds for an indemnity basis costs order (and enhanced interest rates).

**9.** Applications for interim injunctions in defamation claims are in an exceptional category and are not governed by the *American Cyanamid* principles where the defendant intends to rely on, for example, justification (see the **Civil Litigation Manual** at **14.3.3.4**). Answer [A] is wrong because it outlines the *American Cyanamid* principles. Answer [D] identifies the wrong exceptional category. The principles based on Article 10(1) of the European Convention on Human Rights (referred to at **14.3.3.4**) do not apply where the *Bonnard v Perryman* [1891] 2 Ch 269 principle results in the refusal of the injunction (see *Greene Associated Newspapers Ltd* [2005] QB 972). Answers [B] and [C] both point to the reason (protection of free speech) and the effect of the rule in defamation cases, the difference between them being as to whether the defendant's assertion of an intention to justify can be challenged. As made clear at **14.3.3.4**, an injunction may be granted despite the defendant's protestations if the alleged libel is obviously untrue, so the correct answer is [B].

**10.** Robert's problem is that he would like to sue the persons responsible for ramming his boat, but he does not know who they are. He believes that Vincent, who is a local person and who was apparently present when his boat was hit, will know who was responsible. Pre-action disclosure (answer [A]) is only available against a likely defendant, so is not available against Vincent as Robert has no cause of action against him. However, a *Norwich Pharmacal* order can be made against such a person for the purpose of obtaining full information as to the identity of the wrongdoer provided the witness got 'mixed up' in the wrongdoing so as to facilitate its commission. The other boat rammed Robert's boat without any help from Vincent, who was merely painting the harbour. Vincent is therefore a mere witness, and the correct answer is [D]. There is no question of self-incrimination on the facts.

**11.** This question involves the interrelation of two principles in the context of applications for summary judgment. If Peter, the landlord, had sued David, the tenant, simply for the arrears of rent, David would have had a set-off by virtue of his counterclaim for damages for breach of covenant in the lease, see *British Anzani (Felixstowe) Ltd v International Marine Management (UK) Ltd* [1980] QB 137 (see the **Civil Litigation Manual** at **12.7.3**). As the rent arrears are £6,000 and the set-off is worth £4,000, David has no defence for the balance (£2,000), so the district judge would have entered judgment for Peter in the sum of £2,000 and refused the application as to the balance, answer [C]. However, David has given Peter a cheque for £6,000 and dishonoured it. Peter has wisely chosen to sue on the cheque, not for the rent. Under the so-called cheque rule the court will disregard defences and set-offs in relation to the underlying transaction, will enter judgment for the full amount of the dishonoured cheque, and will not even grant a stay of execution (see the **Civil Litigation Manual** at **12.7.4**). None of the limited defences to cheque actions listed at **12.7.4** applies on the facts of this case, so the district judge will enter judgment for £6,000, answer [B].

NB

**12.** In order to answer this question correctly you need to have sufficient knowledge of the special disclosure rules in the Supreme Court Act 1981 so that you are able to identify the correct type of application to make, and you also need to know about the procedure on making such applications. Isaac is suing Highbury: he has no cause of action against the Department for Work and Pensions, who hold the documents he wants to see. Being a non-party, it is not possible to seek an order for pre-action disclosure under the Supreme Court Act 1981, s 33(2) (or its county court equivalent, the County Courts Act 1984, s 52(2)). Answer [C] is therefore wrong. An order for disclosure against a non-party may be made after proceedings have been commenced against the defendant (here Highbury) under the Supreme Court Act 1981, s 34(2) (or the County Courts Act 1984, s 53). At one time there was a requirement that the claim had to be one in respect of personal injuries or death, but this was abolished in April 1999, so answer [D] is wrong. The difference between [A] and [B] turns on whether the application is made by issuing a separate Part 8 claim (which is a form of originating process) or interim application notice. The CPR rr 23.3, 25.1 to 25.3 and 31.17 specify the latter, so the correct answer is [A].

**13.** Under the old system there were express provisions enabling a court to make orders: for further and better lists (answer [B]); for verification of a list of documents by affidavit (answer [C]); and for specific discovery (also known as particular discovery, answer [D]). Under the CPR, verification by affidavit has disappeared and is replaced by a general requirement that lists of documents must contain disclosure statements (CPR r 31.10(5) and PD 31, para 4). As this is incorporated into the list itself, there is no scope for a separate verifying affidavit being ordered on a later occasion. The procedure for ordering further and better lists simply has not been retained by the Civil Procedure Rules. Instead, where a party alleges the other side has given inadequate disclosure, redress may be sought only by seeking an order for specific disclosure (or specific inspection), see PD 31, para 5.1 and CPR r 31.12 and the **Civil Litigation Manual** at **20.7.2**. The correct answer is therefore [D].

**14.** This short question is in fact very difficult. All four answers concern entering judgment in default. Answer [D] contains a common misapprehension that judgment in default can only be entered on the defendant's failure to acknowledge service, whereas the triggering event may be failing to file a defence. The answer is also wrong because the 14 days runs from service of the particulars of claim (which may or may not be indorsed in the claim form).

The correct answer is [B], which sets out the rule that a default judgment will be set aside as of right where any of the conditions in CPR r 12.3(1) or 12.3(7) are not satisfied, as set out in the **Civil Litigation Manual** at **6.2** and **6.7.1**, and CPR r 13.2. These include cases where judgment is entered less than 14 days after service of the particulars of claim. The special rule in CPR r 12.10, that permission is required to enter judgment in default after service outside the jurisdiction without permission under the Jurisdiction Regulation is set out in the **Civil Litigation Manual** both at **6.4.2**, and at **11.8**. Answer [A] is therefore wrong because it says judgment in default in these circumstances may be entered *without* permission. The principal question when considering setting aside a regular default judgment is the question of the merits of the defence (see **6.7.2** and *Thorn plc v McDonald* [1999] CPLR 660, CA), not the explanation for failing to acknowledge service (as stated in answer [C]): it is clear that this is merely a secondary factor.

**15.** Insisting that the applicant merely had to show a serious issue to be tried on the merits was the main point of the *American Cyanamid* decision (see the **Civil Litigation Manual** at **14.3.1**). Consequently the correct answer is [A]. Before *American Cyanamid* the accepted principle was that a party seeking an interim injunction had to establish a prima facie case on the merits of its claim, answer [B]. This often meant the parties felt constrained to attempt to prove the merits of the claim and defence in voluminous affidavits and exhibits, resulting in very long and expensive interim hearings. Avoiding such a waste of resources before trial was the main motivation behind the *American Cyanamid* decision. Answers [C] and [D] are also concerned with the standard of proof, but put the test too high.

**16.** This is a procedural point in relation to claims commenced by the alternative procedure in CPR Part 8. Each time it has appeared in previous MCTs many students have got it wrong. Under the CPR, r 8.5(2), the claimant's evidence must be served with the claim form, so the correct answer is [A]. The evidence should have been filed at court when the claim form was filed (CPR r 8.5(1)). See the **Civil Litigation Manual** at **3.13**.

**17.** Despite the simple form of questions like the present one, they often cause significant difficulties. Before attempting to answer it, it is important to note that it asks for the INCORRECT proposition among the four possibilities. Under the Civil Procedure Rules summary judgment is available in all types of cases except residential possession cases and admiralty claims *in rem* (r 24.3). [A] is therefore not the answer to this question. [B] has been the most popular wrong answer (occasionally attracting more candidates than the proper answer to this question). There is nothing to prevent an application for summary judgment for an injunction if there is no defence with a real prospect of success (see *Cadogan v Muscatt* The Times, 15 May 1990, CA). Probably those who selected this answer thought the only way of obtaining an injunction was by trial or on an *American Cyanamid*-style interim application. Evidence in reply (answer [C]) must indeed be served seven days before the return date: CPR r 24.5. One of the options available is for the court to make a 'conditional order' (PD24, para 4), which requires a party to pay money into court or to take a specified step in the proceedings, with dismissal or striking out in default. If the condition is the payment of money, once the money is paid into court the effect is to give the claimant security in the amount paid in (*Re Ford* [1900] 2 QB 211 and **12.7.2** of the **Civil Litigation Manual**), so the money paid in is *not* part of the defendant's general assets on his bankruptcy. [D] is therefore the INCORRECT answer that should have been selected.

**18.** Dennis must either acknowledge service or file a defence within 14 days of the deemed date of service of the particulars of claim, otherwise he will be at risk of judgment in default being entered: CPR rr 10.3, 12.1, 15.3 and 15.4. Answer [A] is wrong because it provides no guard against this. The purpose behind filing an acknowledgment of service is to 'buy' an extra 14 days for filing the defence (CPR r 15.4 and notes in the Response Pack, Form N9). (The Response Pack is included in the forms enclosed with a claim form when it is served.) Although the court has power to extend time (answer [B] and CPR r 3.1(2)(a)) there is express provision dealing with this situation in CPR r 26.4. This rule provides that the court will stay the proceedings for a month, or such specified period as it considers appropriate, for negotiation if all the parties make a request to that effect in their allocation questionnaires or if the court of its own initiative considers a stay would be appropriate. This is in fact the first question in the allocation questionnaire. There is no need to use an application notice (Answer [D]). Therefore, although answers [B] and [D] are not completely wrong, the best answer is [C], which follows the procedure contemplated by the rules for this situation.

**19.** It is easy to go wrong on this question by not reading it carefully enough. You are asked to identify the proposition that 'best' describes the relevance of the fact the building work has not yet commenced. There are elements of truth in all the answers. Careful reading and a sound understanding of the *American Cyanamid* principles will show that one answer is clearly better than the others. The state of the building work is clearly part of the factual background, but, as will be seen from what follows, it *does* have further relevance to the issues to be considered by the court, so answer [A] is wrong. The court has to consider what the claimant is seeking to injunct and the likely effects on the parties of the defendant's conduct/the proposed order in deciding whether damages will be an adequate remedy, but this is not 'the only relevance' of the fact in question. Answer [B] is therefore an incomplete answer. There is a similar problem with answer [D]. As the work has not started the injunction will be prohibitory. If the work had been completed the injunction would have compelled Lynn to demolish the building, and would have been mandatory. (Different principles apply depending on whether the proposed injunction is prohibitory or mandatory.) Answer [C] is not worded in a restrictive way, unlike answers [A], [B] and [D]. In *American Cyanamid*, Lord Diplock said that where other factors are evenly balanced, it is a counsel of prudence to seek to preserve the status quo (see the **Civil Litigation Manual** at **14.3.1.5**), and hence [C] is the best answer.

**20.** It is first necessary to identify the nature of the order that has been obtained. Being an injunction restraining Claude from removing assets from the jurisdiction, it is a freezing injunction. Note that you are asked to identify the 'best' advice. Answer [A] may have attractions for the dishonest, but would result in Claude being in contempt of court, so is not advice that can be given to him. The Bar Standards Board Conduct Committee would not be impressed if this was your answer! There are elements of truth in answers [B] and [C]. Once a judge learns that the defendant has been notified of the claim, and particularly when the defendant has been notified that the claimant wants some form of security for its damages, the judge may well feel it is inappropriate for a freezing injunction to be sought without notice. Applications made without notice to the other parties are always exceptional, and the matters mentioned in [B] and [C] may incline some judges into refusing to grant a freezing injunction without notice. In such cases the claimant is forced into seeking the relief (if at all) after giving notice of the application to the defendant. However, these are not reasons for *discharging* the order if the judge nevertheless decides to hear the application without notice. The best answer is [D]. A freezing injunction should only be granted where the defendant is the type of person who would dissipate his assets in order to frustrate any judgment the claimant may obtain (see the **Civil Litigation Manual** at **15.3.4**). Note the rather non-legal phrase used in answer [D] to describe this.

**21.** This is a claim for damages for breach of contract. It does not come within the terms of any of the published pre-action protocols (see the **Civil Litigation Manual** at **2.2** and Practice Direction Pre-Action Protocols, para 5.1). There is no such thing as the 'Commercial

Litigation Pre-Action Protocol', so answer [A] is a complete fabrication. In cases like this one where no specific protocol applies, the parties are required to adopt a reasonable pre-action procedure aimed at enabling each side to obtain information about the other side's case, and encouraging them to seek to find a negotiated settlement of the dispute (Practice Direction Pre-Action Protocols, paras 4.1 and 4.2 and see the **Civil Litigation Manual** at **2.3**). This position is summarised in answer [B], which is correct. Answer [C] incorrectly says there are no constraints in cases not governed by a specific pre-action protocol. Answer [D] (which might have been right if the limitation period was about to expire) is wrong because the limitation period for breach of contract claims is six years, which means there are two years left before limitation expires, so there is plenty of time to comply with the ethos of the pre-action protocols.

**22.** Although Karen was ready to exchange witness statements on the date directed by the court, Peter was not. To avoid giving Peter the tactical advantage of seeing her witness statements before he serves his, Karen has decided not to disclose her witness statements. Eight months have elapsed. There have been no previous applications to enforce compliance, so there is no existing 'unless order'. As this is therefore the first occasion on which the court is being invited to enforce compliance, and as no trial date has been fixed (which may result in a harsher response from the court), it is unlikely that the claim will be struck out. It would be different if the delay had resulted in the claim not being capable of being tried fairly (which is particularly important given the terms of Article 6(1) of the European Convention on Human Rights), see *Blackstone's Civil Practice* at para 46.14. The general approach to the imposition of sanctions is discussed in the **Civil Litigation Manual** at **28.3.2**. The correct answer is therefore [A].

Regarding the other answers, although eight months is a protracted delay, answer [B] is not the most likely approach (which is the way it is put in the question) because it is very unlikely that the claim will be struck out. Answer [C] sets out a far too lenient approach. Although it is unlikely that the claim will be struck out, the court will seek to impose a proportionate sanction for Peter's delay, probably in costs, and possibly by one of the other orders listed in *Blackstone's Civil Practice* at para 46.10. There is no obligation on Karen to disclose her witness statements if Peter is unable or unwilling to reciprocate, answer [D]. The direction in this question is for the usual 'exchange' of witnesses' statements, so Karen did not breach the direction by failing to disclose her statements on a unilateral basis.

**23.** This question asks for a ground for making an interim payment. Answer [A] (insurance) is an additional element under the ground set out in CPR, r 25.7(1)(e), but is not in itself a ground for making an interim payment award. Answer [B] (establishing a need for the money) may be relevant to the exercise of the discretion, but is not in itself a ground for doing so. The grounds for ordering an interim payment are set out in CPR r 25.7 (see the **Civil Litigation Manual** at **13.2.1**), and include cases where the claimant has obtained judgment for damages to be decided by the court (see r 25.7(1)(b)). Answer [C] is therefore the correct answer. Answer [D] comes close to stating a ground for granting an interim payment (see r 25.7(1)(c)), and even includes the point made in the **Civil Litigation Manual** at **13.2.3** that set-offs and counterclaims have to be taken into account in applications on the ground set out in r 25.7(1)(c). However this answer omits the key point in r 25.7(1)(c) that the claimant must satisfy the court that if the claim went to trial 'the claimant would obtain judgment' for a substantial amount of money. By stating only half the requirement of this ground, answer [D] is incorrect.

**24.** In this question the deemed date of service is given. Acknowledging service prevents the claimant from entering a default judgment on the expiry of 14 days from the deemed date of service, so answer [C] is incorrect. Track allocation in ordinary county court claims follows filing of a defence, which has not happened yet, and takes place after the parties file their allocation questionnaires, so answer [D] is wrong on two counts. That narrows the question down to finding the expiry of the time for filing a defence following the filing of an acknowledgment of service. Both answers [A] and [B] recognise that the relevant period is 14 days, but acknowledging service adds another 14 days to the period from the deemed date of service of the particulars of claim (so answer [B] is correct), rather than restarting the clock from the date the acknowledgment was filed (answer [A]). See CPR r 15.4(1)(b) and the **Civil Litigation Manual** at **4.4**.

**25.** In questions like this one it is often useful to compile a short chronology:

| | |
|---|---|
| July 2000 | Accrual of cause of action |
| May 2006 | Service of proceedings |
| July 2006 | Expiry of limitation period |
| August 2006 | Service of defence |
| December 2006 | Today |

It will be noticed that the entry for July 2006 is calculated from the date given for accrual of the cause of action. Richard's proposed amendment is to change the company being sued, and is being sought after the expiry of the limitation period. Generally new parties cannot be substituted after the expiry of the limitation period: Limitation Act 1980, s 35(3). However, substitution may be allowed after the expiry of the limitation period if it is necessary for the determination of the original claim (Limitation Act 1980, s 35(5)(b)), and substitution may be regarded as necessary if the original party's name was given in mistake for the new party's name (Limitation Act 1980, s 35(6)(a)). CPR r 19.5(3)(e), which is discussed in the **Civil Litigation Manual** at **24.7.3.4**, is not interpreted restrictively and is intended for putting things right when a mistake has been made (*Morgan Est (Scotland) Ltd v Hanson Concrete Products Ltd* [2005] 1 WLR 2557). Hence the answer is [A]. Answer [C] reflects the general rule in the Limitation Act 1980, s 35(3), but ignores s 35(5) and (6). The other answers were all dreamed up for the MCT. Despite the complexity of the above answer, this is a reasonably straightforward question.

**26.** This question requires knowledge of the bases of assessment of costs. Answer [A] describes the indemnity basis. Answer [B] has been dreamt up, but has its attractions because of the general discretionary nature of costs *orders*. Answer [C] describes the statutory protection on costs of publicly funded parties by virtue of the Access to Justice Act 1999, s 11(1). The correct answer is [D], see CPR r 44.4(1) and (2), discussed in the **Civil Litigation Manual** at **36.5.5**. The proportionality concept is one of the practical applications of the overriding objective in CPR r 1.1.

**27.** The old rules on enforcement continue in operation by virtue of CPR Part 50 (although some of the rules were replaced from March 2002). When answering this question it is first necessary to identify the type of enforcement procedure being described in the answers, and then to consider the mechanics of how they are operated. Answer [A] is the warrant of execution; [B] is the warrant of delivery; and [D] is the warrant of possession. All of these are enforced by the bailiff. Answer [C] describes the third party debt order, which, when made absolute, requires a third party who owes money to the judgment debtor to pay that money to the judgment creditor. This does not require the intervention of the bailiff. Consequently [C] is the correct answer.

**28.** Chronology:

| | |
|---|---|
| June 2003 | Julia injured at work |
| November 2004 | Julia consulted solicitors |
| May 2006 | Claim form issued |
| June 2006 | Limitation expired |
| | Negotiations |
| September 2006 | Validity of claim form expired |
| December 2006 | Today |

Originating process for service within the jurisdiction is valid for the purposes of service for an initial period of four months.

The expiry of the four-month period of validity (in September 2006) is stated as a given fact in the question. From that basis this question asks what additional advice should be given to the claimant, Julia. Answer [A] is to the effect that as the initial period of validity has expired the court no longer has power to grant an extension. Under CPR r 7.6(3) an extension may be sought even after the claim form has expired, provided the court was unable to serve the claim form, or the claimant has taken all reasonable steps to serve, but has been unable to do so (see the **Civil Litigation Manual** at **25.2.2**). Although it is possible to seek the renewal of the claim form, an order should be refused, because Julia cannot satisfy either of the conditions in r 7.6(3) (see *Kaur v CTP Coil Ltd* (2000) LTL 10/7/2000, CA, *Godwin v Swindon BC* [2002] 1 WLR 997 and **25.2.3**). Thus, answer [B] is incorrect.

Answers [C] and [D] both start with the correct proposition that the existing claim form should not be renewed (because of the exacting conditions in r 7.6(3)). Answer [C] states the law on the Limitation Act 1980, ss 11 and 33 as interpreted by the House of Lords in *Walkley v Precision Forgings Ltd* [1979] 1 WLR 606. This case decided that there is no jurisdiction to exercise the discretion under s 33 to 'disapply' the three-year limitation period laid down by s 11 in respect of a second claim where the claimant had issued a first claim within the three-year limitation period. This might arise where the first claim was not served during its four-month period of validity, whether through neglect or to avoid derailing negotiations. *Walkley v Precision Forgings Ltd* proceeded on the basis that, in such cases, the claimant was not prejudiced by the effect of s 11 (as required by s 33), but by failure to proceed with the first claim.

This view has been decisively rejected by *Horton v Sadler* [2006] 2 WLR 1346. In this case, the House of Lords applied *Practice Statement (Judicial Precedent)* [1966] 1 WLR 1234 and departed from *Walkley v Precision Forgings Ltd* as wrongly decided. Under s 33, the relevant claim is the second one and there are no technical restrictions on when the court may exercise its discretion under s 33 to allow a personal injuries claim to proceed despite missing the three-year limitation period. Rather, as s 33 provides, the court has a wide discretion, which may be exercised where it is equitable to do so based on the balance of prejudice between the two parties. It is not necessarily easy to persuade the court to exercise its discretion, but the court does have the power to do so, as set out in answer [D].

Although there is a theoretical possibility of getting an order dispensing with service, this is only realistic if an attempt to serve has been made which ends up being slightly late by reason of the deemed dates of service rules (*Anderson v Clwyd County Council (No 2)* [2002] 1 WLR 3174). This will not apply on the facts, and does not affect the answer.

**29.** The requirement that the claimant's cause of action must be justiciable in England and Wales (see the **Civil Litigation Manual, 15.3.1**) is not of direct relevance to this question, despite the superficial appearance that it is. The question in fact turns on the principles developed by the courts on the requirement that there be a real risk that the defendant in an application for a freezing injunction may dispose of, or dissipate, assets to frustrate any judgment the claimant may obtain, see **15.3.4**. There is no absolute rule that European Union defendants are immune to freezing injunctions, and clearly the Supreme Court Act 1981, s 37(3) and the Civil Jurisdiction and Judgments Act 1982, s 25 militate strongly against any such argument. Answer [A] is therefore incorrect. There is no requirement as set out in answer [C] for consent from the courts where the defendant is domiciled, whether in the European Union or elsewhere. The two most popular answers to this question have been [B] and [D].

*Montecchi v Shimco Ltd* [1979] 1 WLR 1180 laid down the proposition that it is relevant to take into account the difficulty in enforcing an English judgment in the defendant's country when deciding whether to grant a freezing injunction. As the **Civil Litigation Manual** points out, this is of particular significance in relation to European Union defendants, because of the ease of enforcing English judgments in other European Union countries under the enforcement provisions in the 1982 Act/Jurisdiction Regulation. The defendant's domicile in an European Union country is not irrelevant (answer [B]), but is a factor to be taken into account as stated in the correct answer, [D].

**30.** Proceedings may be commenced in England against Daisy Bell only if the rules on seeking permission under CPR, r 6.20 are satisfied. There is therefore no 'absolute right' to use the High Court in London (answer [A]). The USA is not subject to the Jurisdiction Regulation (Council Regulation (EC) No. 44/2001), so answer [C] is wrong. The facts that the contract is governed by English law and that the English courts have been given jurisdiction provide grounds for granting permission to issue proceedings and to serve outside the jurisdiction (r 6.20(5)) see the **Civil Litigation Manual** at **11.3.2.1**). Although this is not all that is required (see **11.3.2**), there are grounds for seeking permission, answer [B].

**31.** Chronology:

| | |
|---|---|
| Three years ago | Cause of action accrued |
| Seven months ago | Laura served request for further information of the particulars of claim |
| Five months ago | Order to provide the requested information within 21 days |
| About four months ago | Expiry of the 21 days |
| Three years' time | Expiry of limitation period |

Dismissal of a claim on the grounds of inordinate and inexcusable delay (not striking out for abuse of process [C] or discontinuance [D]) under the court's inherent jurisdiction is a pre-CPR concept which probably has not survived. Further, on such an application there were a number of conditions, one being that generally the limitation period must have expired. The limitation period is six years as this is a breach of contract claim, so will expire in three years' time. In addition, striking out as a sanction is generally only imposed where it is no longer possible to have a fair trial. There is nothing in the facts to indicate this applies to this case. Hence answer [B] is not the practical answer.

One way in which the court may control its procedures and ensure that the parties comply with their obligations under the timetable is by imposing a sanction for breach. It does this by making an order and specifying the consequences for non-compliance. This type of order is often referred to as an 'unless' order in that unless it is complied with the adverse consequences will follow. The court has a discretion whether to make an unless order (CPR r 3.1(3)). As the order made five months ago did not specify any consequences for non-compliance, the most appropriate next step is to seek an unless order with a sanction in default (answer [A]).

**32.** The rules on disclosure of witnesses statements have developed over recent years. The original position was that written statements taken by solicitors from potential witnesses in advance of trial were protected from disclosure to the other side or the court by legal professional privilege, answer [D]. Then, some of the specialist courts within the High Court experimented with mutual exchange of witnesses' statements, answer [A]. Later, rules were made covering all High Court and county court claims under which the parties could apply for an order for the exchange of witnesses' statements, answer [C]. More recently mutual disclosure was included among the automatic directions which applied in most county court claims and High Court personal injuries claims. The present position is that mutual exchange of witness statements is one of the usual directions made at the track allocation stage or case management conference, so the correct answer is [B].

**33.** An appeal from a final decision in a multi-track case by a county court circuit judge is to the Court of Appeal, answer [C]. Under the Access to Justice Act 1999 (Destination of Appeals) Order 2000 (SI 2000 No. 1071), the normal route of appeal from a county court circuit judge is to a High Court judge (answers [A] and [B]). Both are wrong, however, because art 4 of the Destination of Appeals Order provides an exception for appeals from final decisions in multi-track cases, which applies on the facts of the question, and which is why answer [C] is correct. Note that it is essential that a direction has been given allocating the claim to the multi-track (see *Clark (Inspector of Taxes) v Perks* [2001] 1 WLR 17).

**34.** Mr Brown's report was obtained and paid for by Paul, and has been disclosed to the defendant. A 'better' report has been obtained for Paul from another expert. Having been disclosed, the defendant is entitled to put the first report in evidence: CPR r 35.11 (see the **Civil Litigation Manual** at **29.9**), so answer [D] is correct. Before disclosure it was protected by legal professional privilege, answer [C]. Answers [A] and [B] are based on concepts from other areas.

**35.** You act for the defendant and want to know the nature of other drugs used by the claimant in addition to your client's drugs. An application for specific disclosure (answer [A]) needs to be supported by evidence (see PD 31, para 5.2), which should specify or describe the documents it is intended to require the claimant to disclose. This might be difficult, as the defendant does not know what drugs the claimant has taken. It would be possible to specify 'all prescription forms', but these will have been given to the chemists, or 'all packaging from drugs taken by the claimant' (which should be held to be documents for the purposes of disclosure), but it is likely that these will not have been retained by the claimant. In any event, if any of the documents are still in her possession they should be in her usual list of documents. The claimant is not a 'non-party' (it is her claim!), so answer [B] is nonsense, and without knowing what drugs she has been using there will be no ammunition for cross-examination (answer [D]). The correct answer is [C]. The defendant wants to find out facts, namely the identities (and quantities) of drugs taken by the claimant, and the service of a request for further information is the procedure for achieving this. The request will take the form of a list of written questions put to the claimant, which she must answer by a date stated in the request (usually about 14 days after service). Answer [C] should be the most obvious answer (note, the question asks for the 'most appropriate' advice, rather than the 'correct' advice). The only other answer with any merit is [A]. As the exercise of some judgment is required to answer this question, the other two options ([B] and [D]) have been deliberately designed so they can readily be ruled out.

**36.** Once an order for a reference to the European Court of Justice has been made the English proceedings are stayed until the European Court has given its preliminary ruling on the question referred to it. Rulings given by the European Court are in a general form, so, although the English court is bound by the ruling, it is left to the

English court to decide the English proceedings in the light of the ruling of the European Court. Hence the answer is [A]. Answers [B] to [D] were dreamt up for the purposes of the MCT.

**37.** Where the court makes an order after a hearing on notice (as here) that does not mention costs, the general rule is that no party is entitled to costs against the other party in relation to that matter: CPR r 44.13(1). There are exceptions to the general rule, which are set out in r 44.13(1A). The exceptions cover granting permission to appeal, granting permission to apply for judicial review and orders made without notice. In these cases, silence on costs means 'applicant's costs in the case'. None of the exceptions apply on the facts. The general rule applies in this case, so the correct answer is [C]. The general rule is mentioned a number of times in the *Practice Directions*, with the obvious implication that the court will make use of this simple expedient as one of the possible sanctions against parties who are not conducting litigation in accordance with the overriding objective or in accordance with the ethos of the rules.

**38.** This question requires the wrong answer to be identified. CPR r 32.18 provides that admissions pursuant to a notice to admit are made for the purposes of those proceedings only (answer [A]). The rule also provides that such admissions shall not be used in favour of any person other than the one who served the notice (answer [C]). Rule 32.18(4) provides that the court may allow a party to amend or withdraw any admissions made in reply to a notice to admit on such terms as the court thinks just (answer [B]). It is a common mistake to think that a notice to admit is a means of forcing the other side either to reply or be deemed to admit the facts in the notice, but the only possible sanction for not replying is in costs. See the **Civil Litigation Manual** at **32.3**. The answer to select was therefore [D].

**39.** On a case management conference the judge will review the steps taken by the parties, decide on the directions that would be suitable, and ensure that all agreements that can be reached between the parties about the matters in issue and the conduct of the claim are recorded, see PD 29, para 5.1. To ensure this is a meaningful exercise the parties must ensure that their representatives at the conference are familiar with the case and have sufficient authority to deal with the issues that are likely to arise: CPR r 29.3(2). This requirement is addressed in PD 29 at para 5.2, which goes on to say that where the inadequacy of the representative or his or her instructions (which is the relevant aspect here) leads to the adjournment of a hearing, it is to be expected that a wasted costs order will be made. The correct answer is therefore [D].

**40.** Where, as here, the claimant sues on two causes of action, the defendant has the choice when paying in of making:

(a) a single global payment in respect of both causes of action; or
(b) individual payments in respect of each cause of action.

(See CPR r 36.6(1) and the **Civil Litigation Manual** at **27.2.3**.) The defendant has a free choice in the matter, but the payment notice must make it clear what the defendant has done. Hence answers [A] and [D] are wrong. When the defendant makes a global payment in (as here), the claimant is generally stuck with it, but is allowed to request clarification and in default of a satisfactory answer can apply for an order that the payment notice be clarified: see the **Civil Litigation Manual** at **27.9.1** and CPR, r 36.9. PD 36, para 6.3 indicates that the modern test is whether there is a need for the notice to be clarified. Accordingly, the correct answer is [B].

**41.** Where an interim application is dealt with in less than a day, the court is empowered, and will usually, make a summary assessment of the costs payable to the party awarded its costs of the interim application. See PD Costs, para 13.2 and the **Civil Litigation Manual** at **10.9**. The application here lasted 30 minutes, so summary assessment would be appropriate, answer [A].

**42.** A party is entitled to serve by fax where the recipient has previously indicated in writing that they are willing to accept service by this method (PD 6, para 3 and see the **Civil Litigation Manual** at **3.7.3.3**). Here Darren is acting through a solicitor. In such cases the necessary willingness may be shown by including a fax number on the firm's printed stationery. Darren's solicitors, like most firms, have done this, so service by fax does not make service defective. Answer [A] is therefore incorrect. Service was after 4 pm, so does not take effect until the next business day (CPR r 6.7 and see the **Civil Litigation Manual** at **3.8**). Answer [B] is therefore incorrect.

Business days exclude weekends (r 6.7(3)), therefore service takes effect on the Monday, and the correct answer is [D] rather than [C].

**43.** The CPR r 32.4(2) (**Civil Litigation Manual** at **30.2**) provides that the court will order the parties to serve witness statements for the witnesses they intend to call at trial. Unless the court orders otherwise, the exchanged statement of a witness shall stand as his evidence in chief (r 32.5(2) and see the **Civil Litigation Manual** at **30.7.1**). Witnesses are only allowed to amplify their statements if the court considers there to be a good reason not to confine them to the contents of their statements (r 32.5(4)). Answers [A] and [B] are wrong because they do not refer to the practice laid down by these rules of asking witnesses to adopt the contents of their exchanged witness statements. Answer [C] is correct because any further details have to be sought during examination-in-chief by non-leading questions. Leading questions (answer [D]) are used in cross-examination, and are generally not allowed in examination-in-chief.

**44.** This is the longest question in the Civil Litigation MCT, and is representative of the longer questions that appear on the MCTs. Do not be surprised to find more than one question of this length on any single paper: they will usually be balanced by shorter questions. A careful analysis of the facts is especially important in questions of this type, and setting out a short chronology is an essential first step.

Chronology:

| | |
|---|---|
| July 2000 | Cause of action accrued |
| April 2006 | Claim form issued |
| May 2006 | Defendant's solicitors informed claim form issued |
| June 2006 | Defendant's solicitors' letter |
| July 2006 | Limitation expired |
| August 2006 | Claim form expired |
| December 2006 | Today |

Surprisingly, simply serving and hoping as referred to in answer [A] *is* an option. Serving the claim form after the expiry of the limitation period and the expiry of its period of validity does not make service a nullity, but merely an irregularity (CPR r 3.10). A defendant who does not take the point will be regarded as having waived the irregularity. However, there is no scope for applying for the irregularity to be cured (see the **Civil Litigation Manual** at **1.4.3**), because r 7.6 is regarded as a self-contained code (*Vinos v Marks & Spencer Plc* [2001] 3 All ER 784, CA). Therefore we need to look at the other answers.

It was established under the old rules that continuing negotiations with nothing more did not constitute a good reason for extending the validity of proceedings: *The Mouna* [1991] 2 Lloyd's Rep 221, CA. The current practice is to look for a very good reason for not serving: *Hashtroodi v Hancock* [2004] 1 WLR 3206. If being marked 'without prejudice', the letter of June 2006 could not be looked at, answer [C] would be correct. However, such communications are in fact looked at in interim applications precisely because they can explain apparent inactivity: *Family Housing Association (Manchester) Ltd v Michael Hyde and Partners* [1993] 1 WLR 354, CA. Answer [D] is wrong because it just considers the need to show a good reason for renewing (here the request to postpone service in the 'without prejudice' letter). On the other hand [B] is correct, because it also considers the requirement of attempted service in CPR r 7.6(3) where the application is made after the expiry of the four-month period of validity of the claim form.

**45.** This question concerns the date of knowledge provisions of the Limitation Act 1980, s 14. In April 2001 William did not know he had been injured. At his medical examination he found out he had a lung injury (which would manifest itself at a later date) which would have justified the institution of proceedings. At that stage he already knew it was due to the chemical escape the previous year, and he always knew the identity of the tortfeasor (his employer). Time therefore began to run in January 2002, answer [B] (or possibly slightly before January 2002, see *Broadley v Guy Clapham & Co* [1994] 4 All ER 439). Knowledge that he had a good legal cause of action, which he obtained after consulting the solicitor (answer [D]), is irrelevant, as expressly provided by s 14.

**46.** Like most summary judgment questions, it is easy to go wrong on this question. By virtue of the Sale of Goods Act 1979, s 53, a defendant being sued for the price of goods sold is entitled to set-off a counterclaim for damages in respect of the breach of the conditions implied by the Act, including the implied term as to satisfactory quality. We are told the facts are not in dispute, so the district judge will almost certainly act on the facts set out in the evidence. We are told the counterclaim is worth £2,500. Therefore there is no defence to the balance between the price of £4,000 and the value of the counterclaim, £2,500, which means judgment should be entered for Sally in the sum of £1,500. PD 24, para 5.1 says the orders a court can make on a summary judgment application are:

(a) judgment on the claim;
(b) striking out or dismissal of the claim;
(c) dismissal of the application; and
(d) conditional order.

Paragraph 5.2 has a note which says that the court will not follow the former practice of granting a defendant leave to defend, whether conditionally or unconditionally. So far as this question is concerned, the greatest omission is the lack of any express provision indicating how the court should deal with a summary judgment application where there is no defence to part of the claim but a reasonable defence as to the balance. However, PD 26, para 7.4(2) expressly refers to summary judgment for part of a claim. The best view therefore is that the court can make a 'split' order in cases like this one, with the order being similar to the form set out in answer [C].

**47.** This question needs careful thought. The Master has indicated that the defendants' case is marginally stronger than the claimants'. Prospects of success on a security for costs application should only be taken into account where one side's case is clearly stronger than that of the other. Otherwise applications for security for costs will degenerate into detailed enquiries into the merits, see *Porzelack KG v Porzelack (UK) Ltd* [1987] 1 WLR 420. Consequently, answers [B] and [D] are wrong. Answer [C] is wrong because the claimant's insolvency is not the only factor to be taken into account. Answer [A] is the best answer because it gets the principle correct on the question of the merits of the respective claims, and also takes into account other relevant factors (defendants' conduct contributing to claimant's insolvency and stifling a genuine claim (the merits of the claimants' claim have to be considered, despite what has been said above, for this more limited purpose)). Notice that the way the Master decides this case (whether to grant or refuse security for costs) does not affect the correctness or otherwise of answers [A] and [D] given the way in which they are phrased. This is inevitable in an area, like this one, where the court has a very wide discretion.

**48.** Careful analysis is required for this question. You act for the claimant. You have been successful, and want to get your costs from the publicly funded defendant. You cannot get your costs from the Legal Services Commission under the Access to Justice Act 1999, s 11, answer [D], because the proceedings, which were at first instance, were *not* instituted by the publicly-funded person (Community Legal Service (Costs Protection) Regulations 2000 (SI 2000/824)). [C] is wrong because Martin is protected from the usual costs order by the Access to Justice Act 1999, s 11. [B] is wrong because the protection is not absolute. The usual order made in these circumstances is that stated in answer [A], which gives the successful party, Laura, her costs, but only after the court has determined whether Martin should pay anything under the Costs Protection Rules. See **Civil Litigation Manual** at **35.7.8**.

**49.** The established safeguards for defendants relating to the execution of search orders are set out in the **Civil Litigation Manual** at **16.5.3.2**. A standard form of order is laid down in the Annex to PD 25. The supervising solicitor needs to be someone familiar with the workings of search orders, but there is no need for that person to be a senior partner, and they should not be a member of the firm retained by the claimant (answer [A]). The supervising solicitor is required, among other things, to inform the defendant of his or her right to seek legal advice (answer [C], which is the correct answer), but there is no requirement that the order must be executed in the presence of the defendant's solicitors (answer [B], the presence of an undertaking to this effect making no difference). Answer [D] is wrong because the numbers involved in the 'search parties' must be set out in the order (see **Civil Litigation Manual**, **16.5.3.1**).

**50.** Christopher is at the moment the sole defendant. He wishes to make claims against a non-party, Mary, for a contribution towards any liability he might have to the claimant, and he also wants to claim damages in his own right against her. Nothing is said in the question about making his own damages claim against the claimant and Mary, so the possibility of using a counterclaim against the claimant and bringing in Mary as a defendant to counterclaim can be ignored (answer [D]). The practice of simply writing to inform a joint tortfeasor that a contribution will be sought (rather than issuing a formal notice to that effect) applies only to joint defendants and where the claim between the existing defendants is limited to seeking a contribution pursuant to the Civil Liability (Contribution) Act 1978. Neither of these conditions is satisfied here, so [C] is wrong too. Although issuing separate proceedings (answer [B]) is a possibility, it is not the only one, and it would be more natural to issue an additional claim under Part 20 against the non-party. Answer [B], which uses the word 'must', fails to recognise that there are options, whereas answer [A], which uses the word 'should', does. Further, issuing an additional claim is the sensible option as this has the effect of bringing all the parties to the accident before the court at the same time, removing the risk of irreconcilable findings between the various parties.

**51.** [A], [C] and [D] are all exceptions to the rule of finality of answers to collateral questions. As to [A], bias, see, eg, *Thomas v David* (1836) 7 C & P 350. As to [C], previous convictions, see s 6 of the Criminal Procedure Act 1865, which applies to civil as well as criminal proceedings. As to [D], physical or mental disability affecting reliability, see *Toohey v Metropolitan Police Commissioner* [1965] AC 595. [B] is an 'invented' exception to the rule – there is no common-law or statutory authority to support it.

**52.** [B] is correct. The general rule governing the incidence of the legal burden in civil cases is that he who asserts must prove. Larry is alleging breach of covenant and therefore he must prove Teresa's failure to pay the rent and clean the windows. See *Soward v Leggatt* (1836) 7 C & P 613, where the plaintiff landlord alleged that the tenant 'did not repair' the house and the defendant alleged that he 'did well and sufficiently repair the house'. It was held that the plaintiff had to prove the alleged breach of covenant. Teresa does not bear a legal burden in relation to the alleged breaches of covenant simply by denying them. However, she does bear the legal burden to prove termination of the tenancy by agreement, because it is a defence which goes beyond a simple denial of Larry's assertions. She is asserting such termination and therefore she must prove it.

**53.** The general rule as to the incidence of the legal burden in civil cases is that he who asserts must prove. Is Marcus asserting that it *was* reasonably practicable to keep the premises safe, or are 5-X asserting that it was *not* reasonably practicable to keep the premises safe? The identical issue arose in *Nimmo v Alexander Cowan & Sons Ltd* [1968] AC 107, a Scottish civil case in which a majority of the House of Lords held that the defendant employers bore the burden of proving that it was not reasonably practicable to make and keep the premises safe, since on the face of the statute the incidence of the burden was unclear and the court, in determining Parliament's intention, could go beyond the form of the enactment and look at policy considerations and the ease or difficulty that each of the parties would face in discharging the burden. Since 5-X bear the legal burden on the issue, then in accordance with the general rule they also bear the evidential burden on that issue. [C] is therefore the correct answer.

**54.** This question concerns the admissibility of evidence of bad character relevant to a fact in issue in civil proceedings. The facts of the question are the same, in principle, as those of *Mood Music Publishing Co Ltd v De Wolfe Publishing Ltd* [1976] Ch 119, a claim concerning infringement of copyright in which the defendants alleged that the similarity between the work which they had produced and the work in which the plaintiffs owned the copyright was coincidental. The Court of Appeal held that evidence to show that on other occasions the defendants had produced works bearing a close resemblance to other works which were the subject of copyright was admissible to rebut the allegation of coincidence. [C] is therefore the correct answer.

**55.** [C] is incorrect because in civil cases evidence of the character of a party or a witness may be admissible not only when it is one of the very facts in issue, but also (i) if it is of sufficient relevance to the facts in issue or (ii) if it is sufficiently relevant to credibility (see, eg, the exceptions to the rule of finality of answers to collateral questions). [A] is well established. The exclusion of evidence in civil cases is now governed by CPR, r 32.1 which provides that 'the court may use its power under this rule to exclude evidence that would otherwise be admissible'. It does not provide for the automatic exclusion of evidence because of the way it was obtained. Therefore because of the word, 'solely', [B] is wrong. The authorities to support [D] are *Re Bramblevale Ltd* [1970] Ch 128, CA and *Dean v Dean* [1987] 1 FLR 517, CA.

**56.** This question concerns the standard of proof appropriate to civil cases in which a party makes an allegation of fraud or criminal conduct. The facts of the question are identical, in principle, to those of *Hornal v Neuberger Products Ltd* [1957] 1 QB 247, CA, where it was held that on a charge of fraud, the appropriate standard is proof on a balance of probabilities. Denning LJ said: 'I think it would bring the law into contempt if a judge were to say on the issue of warranty he finds the statement was made, and that on the issue of fraud he finds it was not made.' The answer is therefore [A]. However, he added that: 'A civil court, when considering a charge of fraud, will naturally require for itself a higher degree of probability than that which it would require when asking if negligence were established.' This comment has, understandably, given rise to much confusion. The matter was put more clearly by Ungoed-Thomas, J in *Re Dellow's Will Trust* [1964] 1 WLR 451, when he said: 'The more serious the allegation the more cogent is the evidence required to overcome the unlikelihood of what is alleged and thus to prove it.'

**57.** The authority to support [A] is the Children Act 1989, s 96, whereby a child (a person under the age of 18) who is called as a witness in any civil proceedings but does not understand the nature of an oath *may* be permitted to give unsworn evidence. [D] is well established: the fact that a witness is compellable will not prevent him or her from refusing to answer specific questions if he or she is entitled so to refuse on the grounds of privilege. The authority to support [B], which also illustrates why [C] is incorrect, is the Evidence Amendment Act 1853, s 1 (together with the Evidence Further Amendment Act 1869). Under these statutory provisions, which reversed the common-law rule to the contrary, a spouse of a party to civil proceedings is competent to testify for or against that party.

**58.** [B] is the correct answer because the presumption of continuance of life is a presumption of fact. On the proof or admission of the primary or basic fact (that a person was alive on a certain date) it *may* be presumed, in the absence of sufficient evidence to the contrary, that that person was alive on a subsequent date – establishing the basic fact does *not* have the effect of placing either an evidential or a legal burden on the party against whom the presumption operates. The presumptions referred to in [A], [C] and [D] are all, by contrast, rebuttable persuasive presumptions, whereby on the proof or admission of the primary or basic facts, and in the absence of further evidence, another fact must be presumed, and the party against whom the presumption operates will then bear the legal burden of disproving the presumed fact or, as the case may be, an evidential burden to adduce some evidence in rebuttal of the presumed fact.

**59.** [D] is the correct answer, because each statement is admissible as evidence of any fact stated therein of which direct oral evidence by its maker would be admissible: see Civil Evidence Act 1995, s 1 and s 6(2), s 6(3), s 6(4) and s 6(5).

**60.** A witness in civil proceedings may refresh his or her memory from a document if it was made or verified by the witness at the time of the events it records or so shortly thereafter that the events were still fresh in the witness' memory. The rule applies both to situations where a witness has some recollection of the event but wishes to refresh his or her memory (present recollection revived) and also where the witness has no recollection of the event at all but simply testifies as to the accuracy of the document (past recollection recorded) (see *Maugham v Hubbard* (1828) 8 B & C 14). [A] is therefore correct and [B] and [D] incorrect. In either situation, the memory-refreshing document does not itself become evidence in the case but rather the evidence is the testimony of the witness. [C] is therefore incorrect.

**61.** This question concerns proof of an oral hearsay statement. Section 1(1) of the Civil Evidence Act 1995 provides for the admissibility of hearsay evidence in civil proceedings, and references to hearsay include hearsay of whatever degree, ie, first-hand, second-hand or multiple hearsay: see s 1(2)(b). Quentin's statement, therefore, may be proved by Quentin, Robert, Sylvia or Tariq. If the employer calls Quentin, however, he may not adduce evidence of Quentin's previous statement without the leave of the court: see s 6(2). [D] is therefore the correct answer.

**62.** Under s 31(1) of the Theft Act 1968, questions must be answered in proceedings for the recovery or administration of any property, for the execution of any trust or for an account of any property or dealings with property, notwithstanding that compliance may expose the witness (or his spouse) to a charge for an offence under the Theft Act, but the answers may not be used in proceedings for any such offence. [D] is therefore the correct answer.

**63.** [B] is correct (and [A] and [C] incorrect) because David's evidence constitutes statements of opinion by him on relevant matters (speed, distance, and the suddenness of braking) on which he is not qualified to give expert evidence, but which have been made as a way of conveying relevant facts. The evidence is therefore admissible under s 3(2) of the Civil Evidence Act 1972. [D] is incorrect because in civil proceedings admissible non-expert opinion evidence may relate to the ultimate issues in the case. 'Relevant matter', for the purposes of s 3(2), includes an issue in the proceedings in question: s 3(3) of the 1972 Act.

**64.** The letter is inadmissible for the reasons contained in [C] (not [B] or [D]) because provided that there is some dispute, and an attempt is being made to settle it, the courts are prepared to infer that the attempt was 'without prejudice', even if that expression was not actually used: see *Chocoladenfabriken Lindt & Sprungli AG v The Nestlé Co Ltd* [1978] RPC 287, a case which also explains why [A] is incorrect.

**65.** [B] is the best description, because of the Civil Evidence Act 1968, s 11. Under s 11(1), the fact that a person has been convicted of an offence by a UK court shall be admissible to prove, where to do so is relevant to any issue in the proceedings, that he committed that offence; and under s 11(2), if in any civil proceedings a person by virtue of the section is proved to have been convicted of the offence, he shall be taken to have committed it unless the contrary is proved.

**66.** [A] is correct (and [C] incorrect) because the type of legal professional privilege known as 'litigation privilege' enables a client to claim privilege for, inter alia, statements or reports received from potential witnesses (including experts) provided that the dominant purpose of the preparation of the statements or reports was submission to a legal adviser for use in relation to anticipated or pending litigation. If there was another equally important (or dominant) purpose, for example to inform the client about the cause of an accident so as to prevent such an accident in the future, the statement or report cannot be withheld: see generally *Waugh v British Railways Board* [1980] AC 521, HL. There is no authority to support [B] or [D].

**67.** There is no authority to support [A]. Support for [B] is to be found in *Webster v James Chapman & Co* [1989] 3 All ER 939, ChD, but in *Derby & Co Ltd v Weldon (No. 8)* [1990] 3 All ER 762, the Court of Appeal held that the court is *not* required to carry out that balancing exercise. [D] was, for a long time, the correct answer: see *Guinness Peat Properties Ltd v Fitzroy Robinson Partnership (a firm)* [1987] 2 All ER 716, CA, and *IBM Corp v Phoenix International (Computers) Ltd* [1995] 1 All ER 413, ChD. However in *USP Strategies v London General Holdings* [2004] EWHC 373 and *ISTIL v Zahoor* [2003] 2 All ER 252 the test was reformulated to that stated in [C].

**68.** [A] is incorrect because, provided that an expert states the assumed facts upon which his or her opinion is based, he or she need have no personal knowledge of the facts upon which the opinion is based: see *Beckwith v Sydebotham* (1807) 1 Camp 116. Equally, the expert, as a part of the process of forming an opinion, may refer not only to his or her own research, tests or articles, but also to such research and articles etc by others which form part of the general body of knowledge within the relevant field of expertise: see *Davie v Edinburgh Magistrates* 1953 SC 34. [B] is incorrect because in civil proceedings the rule against experts expressing an opinion on the ultimate issues has been abolished by statute: see the Civil Evidence Act 1972, s 3(1) and (3). [C] is also incorrect: see *H v Schering Chemicals Ltd* [1983] 1 WLR 143. For all the above reasons, [D] is correct.

**69.** Section 10 of the Contempt of Court Act 1981 provides that: 'No court may require a person to disclose ... the source of information contained in a publication for which he is responsible, unless it be established to the satisfaction of the court that disclosure is necessary in the interests of justice or national security or for the prevention of disorder or crime.' It is a question of fact whether any given case comes within one of the four exceptions, and the burden of proving 'necessity' is on the party seeking disclosure: *Secretary of State for Defence v Guardian Newspapers Ltd* [1984] 3 All ER 601, HL. Therefore, [B] is the correct answer.

**70.** The statement is admissible under s 3 of the Criminal Procedure Act 1865, which applies to civil as well as criminal proceedings. It provides that a party producing a witness may, if the witness in the opinion of the judge proves 'adverse' (ie hostile), prove that he has made a statement inconsistent with his present testimony. Where such a statement is proved, it is clearly admissible to establish the witness's inconsistency. In civil proceedings, the statement is also admissible as evidence of any fact stated therein: see Civil Evidence Act 1995, s 1, s 6(3) and s 6(5). [B] is therefore the correct answer.

# APPENDIX 4

# NOTE-FORM ANSWERS TO THE CRIMINAL MCT

### CRIMINAL LITIGATION AND SENTENCING

**1.** Since the trial is a summary trial, the answer is contained in Part 37 of the Criminal Procedure Rules. Rule 37.1(1) allows the prosecutor to make an opening speech. Rule 37.1(2) provides that at the conclusion of the evidence for the prosecution, the accused may address the court, whether or not he afterwards calls evidence (so [D] is wrong). Rule 37.1(4) provides that at the conclusion of the evidence for the defence, the accused may address the court if he has not already done so. Thus, the prosecution have the right to make an opening speech, whereas the defence have the right to make either an opening speech or a closing speech. However, r 37.1(5) provides that prosecution and defence may address the court a second time, but only with the leave of the court (so [A] is wrong and [B] is right).

Note that in a trial on indictment, counsel for the defence can only make an opening speech if the defence intend to call evidence as to the facts of the case other than or in addition to the evidence of the accused: *R v Hill* (1911) 7 Cr App R 1. [C] is wrong because the question states that the trial is a summary trial.

**2.** Detention without charge beyond 24 hours may be authorised by a superintendent; however, the superintendent can only authorise detention for a total of no more than 36 hours from the time of the suspect's arrival in the police station (so [B] is wrong). Detention beyond 36 hours may be ordered by a Magistrates' Court, but only to a maximum of 96 hours, so [A] is wrong (Police and Criminal Evidence Act 1984, s 45(1)). After the expiry of the warrant of further detention issued by the magistrates, where the suspect has been in custody for the maximum period of 96 hours, the police must either charge him or release him on bail. The suspect cannot be re-arrested for the offence for which he was previously arrested unless new evidence justifying a further arrest has come to light since his release: Police and Criminal Evidence Act 1984, s 43(19) (so [D] is wrong). [C] is therefore the correct answer.

**3.** Mike is a juvenile; Neville is an adult.

In [A] the adult is charged with aiding and abetting the juvenile to commit an offence (a summary offence, and so the adult has no choice but to be tried in the Magistrates' Court). In such a case, the adult Magistrates' Court may, in the exercise of its discretion, try the juvenile as well as the adult: Children and Young Persons Act 1933, s 46(1)(b); if the adult court does not try the juvenile it will remit him to the Youth Court for trial.

In [C] the adult and the juvenile are charged with separate, but closely connected, offences. Because the charge against one arises out of circumstances which are the same as or linked with the charge against the other, the adult Magistrates' Court has a discretion to try the juvenile as well as the adult: Children and Young Persons Act 1963, s 18(b).

As to [D], where it becomes apparent during the course of the proceedings in an adult Magistrates' Court that a defendant who was believed to be an adult is in fact under 18, the court may, if it thinks fit, complete the hearing: Children and Young Persons Act 1933, s 46(1)(c). If the adult court decides not to carry on with the hearing, the case will be remitted to the Youth Court.

That leaves [B]. The adult and the juvenile are jointly charged with the same offence. The offence is a summary one, and so the adult will have to be tried in the Magistrates' Court. Where an adult Magistrates' Court tries an adult and a juvenile is jointly charged with the adult, the adult court must try the juvenile as well – there is no discretion to remit to the Youth Court: Children and Young Persons Act 1933, s 46(1)(a). [B] is therefore the correct answer.

**4.** Section 7(3) of the Bail Act 1976 provides that a person who has been released on bail and who is under a duty to surrender into the custody of a court may be arrested without warrant by a police officer if the officer has reasonable grounds for believing that he is not likely to surrender to custody. Thus, [C] is the correct answer.

[A] and [B] are both wrong because the officer did have the power to arrest Tom at the railway station. [D] is wrong because it is irrelevant whether or not the original offence is an arrestable offence.

Note that the question does not ask whether the arrest was in fact lawful; it merely asks what principle is to be applied in determining the lawfulness of the arrest.

**5.** The two defendants are charged separately since two separate offences are alleged, and so a single charge would offend the rule against duplicity (see rule 7.3(1) of the Criminal Procedure Rules). If two or more defendants are charged separately but the facts are connected, the charges may be heard together if the justices think fit. If consent to a joint trial is not forthcoming from all parties, the justices should consider the rival submissions and rule as they think right in the overall interests of justice. The justices should ask themselves whether it would be fair and just to the defendants to allow a joint trial. Only if the answer is clearly yes, should they order joint trial. Thus it is a matter for the discretion of the justices whether the defendants are tried separately or together (*Chief Constable of Norfolk v Clayton* [1983] 2 AC 473, at 491–2, per Lord Roskill) and [D] is correct.

**6.** Criminal damage where the value involved is less than £5,000 must be tried summarily: Magistrates' Courts Act 1980, s 22. However, such criminal damage is one of the offences to which s 40 of the Criminal Justice Act 1988 applies (see s 40(3)). Under s 40(1), if such an offence is founded on the same facts (or forms part of a series of offences of the same or similar character) as an indictable offence, a count alleging that summary offence may be included in the indictment along with the count alleging the indictable offence (so [A] is wrong).

In the present case, the criminal damage is founded on the same facts as the indictable offence of burglary (since they arise out of a single incident: *R v Barrell* (1979) 69 Cr App R 250). [D] is therefore correct.

Burglary is triable either way so Frank can elect Crown Court trial in respect of that offence and so [C] is wrong. However, it is a matter for the prosecution whether the criminal damage charge appears on the indictment – the accused has no right to elect trial in respect of it (so [B] is wrong).

**7.** Section 6(5) of the Bail Act 1976 provides that an offence of absconding under s 6 should be dealt with, 'either on summary conviction or as if it were a criminal contempt of court'. In *Schiavo v Anderton* [1987] 1 WLR 79, it was held that a Bail Act offence is an offence which is triable only in the court at which the proceedings in respect of which bail has been granted are to be heard. See also para I.13 of the *Practice Direction (Criminal: Consolidated).*

Frank has been sent to the Crown Court to stand trial. The substantive proceedings will thus be heard in the Crown Court. It follows that the Magistrates' Court has no jurisdiction over the Bail Act offence (so [D] is wrong). In *Schiavo* it was said that the Bail Act offence of absconding is not an indictable offence. It follows that there will not be a jury trial in respect of it (so [B] is wrong). Further, dealing with a Bail Act offence is not one of the situations prescribed in s 74 of the Supreme Court Act 1981 where a Crown Court judge must sit with lay justices; thus, in dealing with a Bail Act offence, the judge sits alone (so [C] is wrong). [A] states the law correctly.

**8.** Normally, a person who pleads guilty in a Magistrates' Court may appeal to the Crown Court only against sentence (and not against conviction): Magistrates' Courts Act 1980, s 108. However, the plea of 'guilty but I have a defence' is an equivocal plea (compare *R v Durham Quarter Sessions, ex parte Virgo* [1952] 2 QB 1, where a guilty plea was rendered equivocal by subsequent mitigation which was inconsistent with the guilty plea). In such a case, the convicted person may appeal against conviction (so [B] is wrong). The proper procedure is for the Crown Court to decide whether the plea was indeed equivocal and, if it was (as is clearly the case in the present problem) it must remit the case for a trial to take place in the Magistrates' Court: *R v Plymouth Justices ex parte Hart* [1986] QB 950. Hence [A] and [C] are also wrong. [D] is correct.

**9.** An adult Magistrates' Court that has convicted a juvenile may grant an absolute discharge, or impose a conditional discharge or a fine (and also make certain ancillary orders, such as binding over a parent or guardian to exercise proper control over the juvenile): s 8(8) of the Powers of Criminal Courts (Sentencing) Act 2000. If none of these sentences are appropriate, the magistrates will remit the juvenile to the Youth Court for sentence, under s 8(6) of the Powers of Criminal Courts (Sentencing) Act 2000 (so option [C] is correct). Option [A] is wrong because there is a power to remit a juvenile from the adult Magistrates' Court to the Youth Court for sentence (s 8(6) of the 2000 Act); option [B] is wrong because the magistrates can pass sentence on a juvenile if their very limited powers of sentencing under s 8(8) of the 2000 Act are appropriate to deal with the case; option [D] is wrong because there is no power to commit a juvenile from the Magistrates' Court to the Crown Court in a case where the provisions of s 91 of the Powers of Criminal Courts (Sentencing) Act 2000 do not apply.

**10.** Under s 10(3) of the Criminal Appeals Act 1968 (as amended by the Criminal Justice Act 2003), an offender who has been committed for sentence to the Crown Court 'may appeal to the Court of Appeal against any sentence passed on him for the offence by the Crown Court' (and so [C] is wrong). Under s 11 of the Act, such appeal requires leave of a single judge of the Court of Appeal unless the Crown Court judge certified that the case was fit for appeal, and so [A] is wrong. [B] is wrong because a certificate from the Crown Court judge is not the only way of obtaining permission to appeal. It follows that [D] is the correct answer.

**11.** A juvenile ought to be tried summarily unless:

(i) the charge is one of homicide;
(ii) he or she is charged jointly with an adult who is to be tried on indictment, and it is in the interests of justice to commit both for trial;
(iii) the offence is one of those covered by s 91 of the Powers of Criminal Courts (Sentencing) Act 2000 (maximum sentence 14 years or more for an adult, or one of certain specified offences, eg, sexual assault under s 3 of the Sexual Offences Act 2003) and the court considers a sentence under that section might be appropriate. (See the Magistrates' Court Act 1980, s 24(1).)

Here the only exception to the general rule that might apply in this case is (iii). The stated maximum sentence is such that the offence of burglary of a dwelling falls within s 91 of the 2000 Act.

It follows that [A] is right. [B] is wrong, as the magistrates have a discretion and must themselves decide whether the offences are too serious for trial in the Youth Court (see *R (C) v Balham Youth Court* [2004] 1 Cr App R (S) 22, *R (H) v Southampton Youth Court* [2005] 2 Cr App R (S) 30 and *R (CPS) v Redbridge Youth Court* (2005) 169 JP 393). [C] is wrong, since a sentence under s 91 would be lawful. [D] is wrong, since juveniles can be tried in the Crown Court for burglary of a dwelling.

**12.** Summary trials can and often do take place in the absence of the defendant. The Magistrates' Court Act 1980, s 11 deals with the situation where the defendant fails to appear. It gives the magistrates a discretion to proceed in his or her absence. If they do proceed, a not guilty plea must be entered.

Hence [A] is wrong in its use of the word 'must' since the magistrates are not obliged to adjourn. [B] is right. They do have a discretion to hear the case on the basis of a not guilty plea. [C] is wrong in its use of the word 'must': they have a discretion on the question of whether to proceed. [D] is wrong, since, if they do proceed, they have no discretion as to the plea – they must deal with the case on the basis of a not guilty plea.

**13.** Under s 36 of the Police and Criminal Evidence Act 1984, the decision to detain must be taken by the custody officer, who should hold at least the rank of sergeant. There must then be periodic reviews of detention – those of relevance here are six hours after the original decision and nine hours after that. The review officer must hold the rank of inspector or above.

[A] is therefore wrong: there was no need to hold reviews at the times stated in that option. [B] is wrong for the same reason. [C] is right; the officer deciding to detain in the first place should have been at least a sergeant; the officer reviewing the detention should have been at least an inspector. [D] is wrong, since Jacob does have a legitimate ground of complaint.

**14.** This question invites you to select the incorrect answer. Appeal by way of case stated (unlike judicial review) does not require the permission of the High Court, so [B] is an incorrect statement and therefore the correct response to the question. Even though a point of law is in issue, an appeal to the Crown Court (under s 108 of the Magistrates' Courts Act 1980) is an option open to the appellant (and the hearing would indeed take the form of a complete re-hearing of the case against him). The fact that the appeal does involve a question of law means that appeal by way of case stated (under s 111 of the 1980 Act) is also available. However, if an appellant invites the magistrates to state a case (the appropriate method of commencing this form of appeal), the right to appeal to the Crown Court is lost (see s 111 (4) of the 1980 Act). Thus, [A], [C], and [D] are all correct statements.

**15.** Where a defendant is convicted by the magistrates and appeals to the Crown Court, sentence falls to be reconsidered, even if the appeal is against conviction only. When reconsidering sentence, the Crown Court can reduce it, leave it unaltered, or increase it to the maximum which the magistrates could have imposed (Supreme Court Act 1981, s 81). The Crown Court can also make such order as to costs as it thinks just.

So [A] is wrong, since the Crown Court has the power to increase sentence. [B] is wrong, since, although the statement as to its powers on sentence is correct, it *can* both increase sentence and order him to pay costs. [C] is correct. [D] is wrong, since the power of the Crown Court to increase sentence is limited to the maximum the magistrates could have imposed and not the maximum applicable to trial on indictment (5 years).

**16.** [B], [C] and [D] indicate circumstances that the court may lawfully take into account: Criminal Justice Act 2003, ss 145 and 146. [A] indicates a circumstance, gender, that is not included in any provision of the Act.

**17.** Disclosure by the defence is governed by the Criminal Procedure and Investigations Act 1996 (as amended by the Criminal Justice Act 2003). Section 6A of the 1996 Act requires the accused to disclose, inter alia, particulars of any alibi (including the name, address and date of birth of any witness the accused believes may be able to give evidence in support of the alibi) and any point of law (including any point as to the admissibility of evidence) which the accused wishes to take. It follows that Martha must disclose all the matters listed in [A], [B] and [C], and so the correct answer to the question is [D].

**18.** Where the jury cannot agree, after all appropriate steps have been taken, the judge will discharge them. The defendant is not acquitted, and may be retried if the prosecution so decide. In practice, it is usual for the prosecution to initiate a second trial. If the jury again fail to agree, the practice is for no evidence to be offered at the start of what would otherwise be the third trial.

[A] is therefore wrong, because it is up to the prosecution to decide and the word 'must' is incorrect. [B] is right. [C] is wrong since the prosecution require no leave to proceed to retrial. [D] is also wrong, since the defendant has not been acquitted.

**19.** This question asks you to identify a sentence that may *not* be imposed. [A] [B] and [C] are incorrect as the court has power to impose custody plus orders, intermittent custody orders and suspended sentence orders, Criminal Justice Act 2003, ss 181(3), 183 and 189. [D] is correct, as there is no provision in the legislation for suspended custody plus orders.

**20.** The court can amend an indictment before or at any stage of the trial, unless the amendment cannot be made without injustice (Indictments Act 1915, s 5). [A] states the law correctly, and is the right choice. [B] is wrong because the counts in the indictment do not need to correspond with those on which the accused was sent for trial, either at the start of the trial or thereafter. [C] is wrong because the indictment can be amended during trial, subject to the limits stated above. [D] is wrong since it is for the court to amend the indictment.

**21.** This is a case where the guilty plea was entered under duress, and the rules relating to equivocal pleas apply (see *R v Huntingdon Crown Court, ex parte Jordan* [1981] QB 857). [A] is wrong since the case will not be reheard in the Crown Court. It will be remitted to the magistrates for hearing on a not guilty plea, as stated in [B], which is the correct choice. [C] is wrong. The magistrates are no longer seised of the matter and, in any event, the case would not be reheard in the Crown Court. [D] is also wrong, since it is the Crown Court rather than the magistrates which should determine that the case should be heard again by the magistrates.

**22.** In certain circumstances, the jury can bring in a verdict of guilty of an alternative offence. The general rule is contained in s 6 of the Criminal Law Act 1967, which states that such a verdict can be returned where the alternative offence is contained, expressly or by implication, in the offence charged. (There are other statutory provisions relating to particular offences, none of which is relevant here.)

[A] is therefore correct. An allegation of robbery includes an allegation of theft, since robbery is theft with additional elements added. [B] is wrong. Theft *is* a less serious offence than robbery, but that is not the reason why the jury can return such a verdict. [C] is wrong because the deletion of particulars can be used to see whether an alternative verdict is *expressly* included in the charge. It does not, however, deal with the other possibility: that the alternative verdict is *impliedly* included in the charge, as it is here. [D] is wrong since alternative verdicts are available in the circumstances specified by, for example, s 6 of the 1967 Act.

**23.** This question seeks the identification of an INCORRECT statement. The case of *R v Goodyear* [2005] EWCA Crim 888; [2005] 1 WLR 2532 gives detailed guidance about indications of sentence by trial judges. The guidance makes it clear that a judge should not give an indication of sentence unless one has been sought by the defence (option [A]), that where an indication is sought, the judge may refuse to give an indication, with or without giving reasons (option [B]), and that once an indication has been given, it is binding and remains binding on the judge who has given it, and it also binds any other judge who becomes responsible for the case (option [D]). Options [A], [B] and [D] therefore set out correct propositions. Option [C] is the correct answer, because it set out an incorrect proposition. The *Goodyear* guidelines say that an indication should not be sought while there is any uncertainty between the prosecution and the defence about an acceptable plea to the indictment, or any factual basis relating to the plea. If an indication is sought in a case of such uncertainty, the judge should therefore decline to give an indication (not give differing indications).

**24.** [A] is correct and [B] incorrect as the maximum aggregate custodial sentence that the Youth Court has power to impose is a detention and training order of 24 months (Powers of Criminal Courts (Sentencing) Act 2000, ss 100 and 101). [C] and [D] are incorrect as the Youth Court only has power to commit the offender to the Crown Court for sentence where a guilty plea has been entered and it is considered that a sentence under Powers of Criminal Courts (Sentencing) Act 2000, s 91 would be appropriate: Powers of Criminal Courts (Sentencing) Act 2000, s 3B.

**25.** An accused whose submission of no case has been wrongly rejected has been deprived of the certainty (rather than the possibility) of an acquittal. The conviction should therefore be quashed, and option [A] is right (see *R v Abbott* [1955] 2 QB 497, *R v Juett* [1981] Crim LR 113, *R v Cockley* (1984) 79 Cr App R 181). In *Smith* [1999] 2 Cr App R 238 it was confirmed that the conviction was unsafe and should be quashed if the submission of no case was wrongly rejected. [A] is therefore correct.

[B] is wrong, both because the accused is entitled to an acquittal, and because the case does not fit within the limited circumstances in which a *venire de novo* is possible (see *R v Rose* [1982] AC 822). [C] is wrong, because the accused would have been acquitted if the judge had ruled correctly. [D] is wrong, both for the reasons already canvassed, and because the Court of Appeal will avoid putting itself in the place of the jury.

**26.** The crucial point here is that the jury have retired. There is an absolute rule that, once the jury have been sent out to consider their verdict, no further evidence may be adduced (*R v Owen* [1952] 2 QB 362]. The right answer, therefore, is [D].

As to [A], the jury can hear additional evidence for the prosecution if the judge gives leave, but only *before* they retire. [B] is excluded by *Owen*. [C] is wrong: the jury may ask questions after retirement.

**27.** [A] and [B] are both wrong, because the High Court's jurisdiction to grant bail in such cases was abolished by s 17 of the Criminal Justice Act 2003. [D] is wrong because, although he could make a further application to the magistrates (if he could demonstrate a change in circumstances), this is not his 'only' option. He may apply to the Crown Court for bail, and so option [C] is correct.

**28.** [B] is incorrect as Criminal Justice Act 2003, s 181(7)(a) provides that the Magistrates' Court may only impose up to a total of 65 weeks in the case of consecutive terms for two or more offences. [C] is incorrect as magistrates cannot exceed 12 months for a single offence. [D] is incorrect for the same reason. [A] is the correct answer. The maximum sentencing power of the magistrates in respect of any one offence is 12 months: Criminal Justice Act 2003, s 154.

**29.** By the Criminal Appeal Act 1968, s 3, the Court of Appeal may in certain circumstances substitute for the verdict of the jury a verdict of guilty of an alternative offence. The power arises when (i) the jury could, on the indictment, have found the appellant guilty of the alternative offence, and (ii) it appears from the jury's verdict that they must have been satisfied of the facts proving the appellant's guilt of the alternative offence.

Theft is an alternative verdict where burglary contrary to the Theft Act 1968, s 9(1)(b) is charged. [C] is on the facts in this question the likeliest course of action. [A] is unlikely, since it appears Daniel was guilty of theft, and the Court of Appeal has the power to substitute a conviction for theft. [B] would clearly be a wrong course to take, since Daniel is not guilty of burglary.

It is unlikely that the Court of Appeal will follow course [D]. The evidence for both prosecution and defence indicates that a retrial will result in a verdict of guilty of theft (rather than not guilty, or guilty of burglary). A retrial should be ordered only where the interests of justice so require (Criminal Appeal Act 1968, s 7(1)).

**30.** The prosecution duty of disclosure is set out in s 3(1) of the Criminal Procedure and Investigations Act 1996. It lays down that the:

'... prosecutor must ... disclose to the accused any prosecution material which has not previously been disclosed to the accused and which might reasonably be considered capable of undermining the case for the prosecution against the accused, or of assisting the case for the accused ... '

It is usual to refer to 'material which has not previously been disclosed' as unused material.

It follows that [D] is the correct answer, because it accurately reflects the law. [A] is insufficiently comprehensive, because it does not include material that might assist Joseph's defence. [B] also fails to include a crucial element of the duty in that it does not include material that might undermine the prosecution case. [C] is wrong because disclosure is obligatory for the prosecution, whether in the Magistrates' Court or the Crown Court. It is the service of a defence statement that is voluntary in the Magistrates' Court.

**31.** Whilst the judge is entitled to use a form of words to encourage the jury to reach a verdict, they must not be subjected to any pressure. The case which lays down the form which such a direction ought to take is *R v Watson* [1988] QB 690. That case approves each of the formulae contained in [A], [B] and [C]. It also expressly rules out any reference by the judge to the unfortunate consequences of a failure to agree, such as cost and inconvenience (overruling *R v Walhein* (1952) 36 Cr App R 167). [D] therefore contains the direction which is forbidden, and it follows that [D] is the correct answer.

**32.** Proviso (i) to s 2(2) of the Administration of Justice (Miscellaneous Provisions) Act 1933 provides that where the accused has been sent for trial, the indictment against him may include, either in substitution for or in addition to any count charging the offence(s) sent for trial, any counts alleging offences that are disclosed in the papers which are sent to the Crown Court, provided that those counts may lawfully be joined in the same indictment. It follows that [A] is incorrect.

But the prosecution may not rely on this proviso to prefer an indictment consisting *entirely* of counts which have not been sent for trial, even where the accused has been sent for trial on other charges and the offences charged in the indictment are disclosed in the papers sent to the Crown Court (*R v Lombardi* [1989] 1 WLR 73). That is what has been done here, and it follows that the trial judge's decision was incorrect for the reason stated in [B], which is therefore the correct answer.

[C] states the law too broadly in view of *Lombardi* and in the light of the words from the proviso referred to above: counts which may lawfully be joined in the same indictment. [D] is wrong, having no basis in law.

**33.** [B] [C] and [D] are available to the court, as these requirements are listed in Criminal Justice Act 2003, s 177 (1)(e), (f) and (j). The correct answer is [A]. Peter is aged 27, and an attendance centre requirement is only available where an offender is aged under 25: Criminal Justice Act 2003, s 177(1)(l).

**34.** [D] is wrong because Susie does have a ground of appeal. Where a defendant pleads guilty but there is a significant difference between the prosecution version of events and the defence version of events (as where the defendant pleads guilty but says that the offence is less serious than the prosecution claim), the judge must either: accept the defence version of events, or hear evidence on the disputed matter and make a finding of fact. Thus, it is improper for the judge to accept the prosecution version without having heard evidence to support that version. See *R v Newton* (1982) 77 Cr App R 13. Where the judge wrongly fails to conduct a *Newton* hearing, the Court of Appeal will allow the appeal and impose the sentence which would be appropriate on the basis of the defence version of events (see, for example, *R v Mohun* (1993) 14 Cr App R (S) 5). Thus the Court of Appeal, in a case such as Susie's, would take the course of action set out in [A], not the course of action set out in [B] or [C].

**35.** The sentence is wrong in law since a defendant cannot be sentenced to a term of imprisonment before the age of 21. The Criminal Appeal Act 1968, s 11 provides that no appeal shall lie against sentence unless either:

(a) the appellant has been granted leave to appeal by the Court of Appeal; or
(b) the trial judge certifies that the case is fit for appeal against sentence.

[A] is therefore wrong. Arnold *does* need leave to appeal. [B] is incorrect, since there are two ways in which an appeal may lie against sentence, and it is not accurate to state that the leave of the single judge of the Court of Appeal is the only one. [C] is similarly wrong because the certificate of the trial judge is not the sole basis on which an appeal can lie. [D] is correct, as the only answer that properly outlines both alternative routes.

**36.** [A] complies with s 8 of the Criminal Justice Act 1967 which provides that the jury, in deciding whether a person has committed an offence: (a) shall not be bound in law to infer that he intended or foresaw a result of his actions by reason only of its being a natural and probable consequence of those actions; but (b) shall decide whether he did intend or foresee that result by reference to all the evidence, drawing such inferences from the evidence as appear proper in the circumstances. None of [B], [C] or [D] complies with s 8. [D] also erroneously suggests that Gareth has the legal burden of disproving the requisite intent.

**37.** [B] is correct (and [C] is incorrect) because under s 10 of the Criminal Justice Act 1967, a formal admission may be made at the proceedings by or on behalf of the prosecutor or defendant, and in court, counsel may formally admit a fact under s 10 *orally*. [A] is incorrect because under s 10(2)(b) it is if the admission is made *otherwise than in court* that it shall be in writing. [D] is doubly incorrect: the formal admission *is* admissible; and even assuming (wrongly) that it is inadmissible, at common law a judge has no discretionary power to admit evidence which is inadmissible in law.

**38.** Ghisha, the wife of the accused Fred, is competent to give evidence for the prosecution: Youth Justice and Criminal Evidence Act 1999, s 53(1). She is not compellable because the case falls outside the Police and Criminal Evidence Act 1984, s 80(2A) and (3), which set out the only circumstances in which the spouse of an accused shall be compellable to give evidence for the prosecution. Irene is also competent by virtue of s 53(1) of the 1999 Act. She is compellable pursuant to the general rule at common law that competent witnesses are also compellable. Her position is not governed by s 80 of the 1984 Act because she is not 'the wife . . . of a person charged in the proceedings' – her husband, Harry, by pleading guilty, has ceased to be such a person (see s 80(4A) of the 1984 Act). [B] is therefore the correct answer.

**39.** [A] is incorrect because, while s 41 of the Youth Justice and Criminal Evidence Act 1999 prohibits cross-examination by (or on behalf of) the accused about the complainant's sexual behaviour in proceedings for sexual offences, it also creates a number of exceptions to the rule. [B] is incorrect because the judge has no power to prohibit cross-examination by the defence on the grounds that the evidence adduced thereby is more prejudicial than probative. [C] is incorrect because where the complainant's sexual behaviour is relevant to an issue other than an issue of consent (Phil's defence is *belief* in consent) the Act does not require that the sexual behaviour and the event that is the subject matter of the charge take place at or about the same time (see s 41(3)(a)). No matter which exception applies under s 41(2)(b) of the Act, the judge must also be satisfied that a refusal of leave might have the result of rendering unsafe a conclusion of the jury or (as the case may be) the court on any relevant issue in the case. [D] is therefore the correct answer.

**40.** [A] is incorrect because s 102 of the Criminal Justice Act 2003 defines 'important explanatory evidence' as evidence without which the court or jury would find it impossible or difficult properly to understand other evidence. Clearly, Nora's allegations can be understood without the evidence of the pornographic magazines. Michael has not raised a defence to be rebutted by such evidence (such as an innocent touching). Michael has completely denied an offence and evidence of his disposition to commit such offences does not rebut a denial (*R v Lewis* (1983) 76 Cr App R 33). Equally, a plea of not guilty is not a 'false impression' because, under s 105(2) of the 2003 Act, the only assertions by the defendant that can amount to 'false impressions' are those made by the defendant in the proceedings or upon being questioned under caution or upon charge. It seems almost certain that this cannot include the fact of pleading not guilty (although the 2003 Act is silent on the point). Section 101(1)(d) states that evidence of bad character can be admissible if 'it is relevant to an important matter in issue between the defendant and the prosecution'. Section 103(1)(a) provides that this includes evidence of a propensity to commit offences of the kind with which he is charged. While it is not certain that this evidence will be admitted, given the restrictions imposed by s 103(1)(a), s 101(1)(d) provides the most appropriate ground for admitting the evidence.

**41.** The general rule is that the prosecution, who bring criminal proceedings against a defendant, bear the legal burden to prove all elements of the offence(s) on which the defendant is tried (*Woolmington v DPP* [1935] AC 462, HL). There are a number of statutory exceptions to this rule and one common law exception (insanity). Self-defence is a common law defence to which the normal rules apply. The defendant therefore bears the evidential burden, the prosecution the legal burden and the standard of proof is beyond reasonable doubt. (See *R v Lobell* [1957] 1 QB 547, CCA.) [A] is therefore the correct answer.

**42.** The facts of this case are, in principle, identical to those of *R v Burke* (1858) 8 Cox CC 44. In that case an Irish witness gave evidence through an interpreter and was cross-examined about his knowledge of English. He denied that he could speak English. It was held that evidence in rebuttal was inadmissible under the rule of finality of answers to questions concerning collateral matters, because his ability to speak English was irrelevant to the matters directly in issue in the case. For this reason, [C] is correct and [A], [B] and [D] incorrect. As to [D], it should be added, it has been said that *where the disputed issue is a sexual one between two persons in private*, the difference between questions going to credit and questions going to the issue is reduced to vanishing point (see per Henry J in *R v Funderburk* [1990] 2 All ER 482, CA, at p 491). NB, this evidence is not governed by the Criminal Justice Act 2003 as fluency in English is not evidence of bad character.

**43.** (i) is possible under s 10 of the Criminal Justice Act 1967. (ii) is possible under s 6 of the Criminal Procedure Act 1865, s 73 of the Police and Criminal Evidence Act 1984 and s 117 of the Criminal Justice Act 2003. As to (iii), s 101 of the Criminal Justice Act 2003 provides for the admissibility of evidence of bad character of the defendant and does not place any qualification upon when in proceedings this may or may not happen. Therefore, unlike the Criminal Evidence Act 1898, which the 2003 Act has replaced, the admissibility of evidence of bad character does not depend upon whether or not the defendant testifies. [D] is therefore the right answer.

**44.** The statement in (i) is correct because the general rule is that a witness may not be asked in examination-in-chief about former statements made by him and consistent with his evidence in the proceedings (see *R v Roberts* [1942] 1 All ER 187). The statement in (ii) is correct because one of the exceptions to the general rule arises if, in cross-examination, it is suggested to the witness that his version of events is a recent invention or fabrication, in which case evidence of a prior statement to the same effect will be admissible, in re-examination, to support his credit (see, eg, *R v Oyesiku* (1971) 56 Cr App R 240, CA). This exception to the general rule of inadmissibility is preserved by s 120(2) of the Criminal Justice Act 2003.

**45.** [A] is incorrect because previous identification of the accused is a well-established exception to the general rule against previous consistent or self-serving statements and is now placed on a statutory footing by s 120(5) of the Criminal Justice Act 2003. [B] is incorrect (and [D] correct) because it is generally undesirable and improper first to invite a witness to identify the accused from the witness box, ie to make a 'dock identification' (see *R v Cartwright* (1914) 10 Cr App R 219); if there has been a previous out-of-court identification of the accused by the witness, the best and usual practice is to elicit evidence of the previous identification *before* then asking the witness whether that person is in the courtroom. However, in *Holland v HM Advocate* [2005] HRLR 25, PC, it was held that there was no basis, except perhaps in an extreme case, either in domestic law or under Art 6 of the ECHR, for regarding dock identifications as inadmissible per se. [C] is incorrect because if the witness cannot give evidence identifying the accused in court, there is no testimony with which the previous identification can be consistent.

**46.** [B] is incorrect because the evidence is clearly relevant to the issue whether Alf's conduct was deliberate or accidental. The admissibility of evidence of propensity to commit offences is now governed by ss 101(1)(d) and 103(1)(a) of the Criminal Justice Act 2003. Section 101(1)(d) provides that evidence of bad character will be admitted if it is relevant to an important matter in issue between the defendant and the prosecution. Section 103(1)(a) provides that an important matter includes evidence of a propensity to commit an offence of the kind with which the defendant is charged. Therefore [A] is incorrect. Pursuant to s 101(3), evidence relevant to an important matter in issue must be excluded if the court is of the opinion that admitting it would have an adverse effect on the fairness of proceedings. Therefore [D] is wrong and [C] is correct.

**47.** Code D3.12 provides that whenever there is a witness available who expresses an ability to identify the suspect, that witness has not been given an opportunity to participate in a video identification, identification parade or group identification and the suspect disputes being the person whom the witness claims to have seen, then an identification procedure must be held unless it is not practicable or would serve no useful purpose in proving or disproving whether the suspect was involved in committing the offence. The question tells us that it would have been practicable for a procedure to have been held. Thus, on the facts, the only circumstance in which the police could refuse to hold one would be where it would serve no useful purpose. The fact that there has been a previous street identification does not negate the obligation in D3.12 (although it may be a factor that could lead the police to conclude that an identification procedure would serve no useful purpose). Whether or not to hold an identification procedure is always the decision of the police and not the suspect (although it is open to the suspect and/or his legal advisor to seek to make representation to the police about doing so). [C] is therefore the correct answer.

**48.** At common law a previous consistent statement is only evidence of the inconsistency of the witness. Under s 119 of the Criminal Justice Act 2003, where a witness gives oral evidence and admits to making a previous inconsistent statement, the statement is also admissible as evidence of any matter stated of which evidence by him would be admissible. As Charles could give admissible evidence of the status of the traffic lights the statement may be relied upon for the truth of the matter stated. [C] is therefore the correct answer.

**49.** Evidence of bad character is not admitted simply to prove that a person is dishonest nor is the fact that evidence of bad character may have this effect enough, on its own, to justify the admissibility of such evidence under the Criminal Justice Act 2003. Therefore [A] is wrong. [B] is wrong because alleging mistaken identity is not an attack upon another person's character under ss 101(1)(g) and 106 of the 2003 Act. While it might be argued that a conviction for indecent exposure might show a general propensity towards sexual offences, it is unlikely that such a conviction would be admissible under ss 101(1)(d) and 103(1)(a) of the 2003 Act as it is strongly arguable that Morgan's conviction makes it 'no more likely that he is guilty of the offence' under s 103(1)(a) and would not therefore be admissible. For this reason [D] is incorrect. The best justification for the admissibility of the evidence is under ss 101(1)(f) and 105 in that the evidence of the previous conviction corrects the false impression created by Morgan in evidence that he had never been in trouble with the police before. The correct answer is therefore [C].

**50.** [A] is incorrect because the common law rules relating to the admissibility of evidence of bad character are abolished by s 99(1) of the Criminal Justice Act 2003. [B] is correct (see *R v Vye* [1993] 1 WLR 471, CA) because, although there is no need for a direction as to the value of good character in assessing the credibility of the accused (as there is no statement or testimony to assess the credibility of), the accused is entitled to have the jury directed that they may take his or her good character into account when deciding whether he or she committed the offence. Both [C] and [D] are wrong because 'character' in the Criminal Justice Act 2003 also includes both reputation (s 118(1)) and disposition (s 98).

**51.** Section 98 of the Criminal Justice Act 2003 defines bad character as, inter alia, evidence of misconduct. Misconduct includes the commission of an offence (s 112 of the Act). Section 99 of the Act abolishes the common law rules governing the admissibility of evidence of bad character in criminal proceedings. Therefore the previous convictions of a person other than a defendant are only admissible under the Act. Statement (ii) is therefore inaccurate. Section 100 of the Act provides that a previous conviction of a person other than the defendant is admissible in three situations:

(a) it is important explanatory evidence;
(b) it has substantial probative value in relation to a matter that:
    (i) is a matter in issue in the proceedings; and
    (ii) is of substantial importance in the context of the case as a whole;

or

(c) all parties to the proceedings agree to the evidence being admissible.

Statement (i) is therefore accurate. Section 100(4) provides that evidence of the bad character of a person other than the defendant must not be given without leave of the court unless the parties agree. Therefore statement (iii) is also accurate. [B] is the correct answer.

**52.** The out-of-court statement allegedly made by Amanda is admissible hearsay: it is a confession as defined in the Police and Criminal Evidence Act 1984, s 82(1) ('any statement . . . adverse to the person who made it') and admissible under s 76(1) of that Act. Concerning a voir dire, where the prosecution intend to rely on an oral confession and the defence case is simply that the accused never made it, no question of admissibility arises for the judge to decide and there is therefore no need for a voir dire. The only issue is a question of fact, whether or not the accused made the confession, and that is for the jury (see *Ajodha* v *The State* [1981] 2 All ER 193, PC, applied in *R* v *Flemming* (1988) 86 Cr App R 32, CA). [C] is therefore the correct answer. It would be otherwise, of course, had Amanda alleged oppression, something said or done likely to render unreliable any consequent confession, or some impropriety (apart from the alleged invention of the confession).

**53.** [D] is correct (and [A] incorrect) because the statement contains facts of which oral evidence would be admissible; and the person who made it is dead (Criminal Justice Act 2003, s 116(1)(a) and (2)(a)). In principle, it is therefore admissible hearsay. [B] is incorrect because the document was not created or received by a person in the course of a trade, business, profession etc (s 117(2)(a)). [C] is incorrect because the statement does not come within one of the three categories of *res gestae*: it was not made in response to an emotionally overpowering event; it did not accompany an act that cannot be evaluated properly without reference to it; and it did not relate to a physical sensation or mental state (see s 118(1) of the 2003 Act).

**54.** At common law, the judge has a discretion to exclude any evidence where its prejudicial effect outweighs its probative value. However, with the exception of admissions, confessions and evidence obtained from the accused after the commission of the offence, evidence may not be excluded at common law solely on the ground that it was obtained by improper, unfair or unlawful means (*R v Sang* [1980] AC 402). Because the judge is of the view that the prejudicial effect of the evidence does not outweigh its probative value and because the evidence does not come within the proviso relating to confessions, there is no common law power to exclude the evidence and [B] and [C] are therefore incorrect. Under s 78 of PACE 1984 the court has a discretion to exclude any evidence where, having regard to all the circumstances, including the circumstances in which the evidence was obtained, the admission of the evidence would have such an adverse effect on the fairness of the proceedings that the court ought not to admit it. This includes a discretion to exclude evidence that has been obtained by improper and unfair means. [A] is therefore the correct answer.

**55.** [A] is incorrect because the conditions of admissibility contained in s 76 apply to a 'confession' and this is defined to include 'any statement ... whether made to a person in authority or not' (s 82(1) of the 1984 Act). [B] is incorrect because under s 76(2)(b) the judge may only rule a confession admissible if, 'notwithstanding that it may be true', he is satisfied beyond reasonable doubt that it was not obtained in consequence of anything done or said etc [C] is correct: s 76(2)(b) requires a causal connection between what was said or done and the confession. Thus if the judge was satisfied that the confession was not obtained 'in consequence of Beatrice's statement', this could have been the justification for his decision to admit it. There is no authority to support [D].

**56.** [B] is correct because where, at a trial on indictment, the case against the accused depends wholly or substantially on a confession by him and the court is satisfied that (i) he is mentally handicapped and (ii) the confession was not made in the presence of an independent person, the court shall warn the jury that there is a special need for caution: see the Police and Criminal Evidence Act 1984, s 77. There is no authority to support [A]. [C] is incorrect: the test of competence in criminal proceedings is whether the person in question is able to (i) understand questions put to him as a witness and (ii) give answers to them which can be understood (Youth Justice and Criminal Evidence Act 1999, s 53(3)). [D] is incorrect because the proper test for giving evidence on oath is not whether the witness understands the divine sanction of the oath, but (i) whether he has attained the age of 14 and (ii) whether he has a sufficient appreciation of the solemnity of the occasion and of the particular responsibility to tell the truth that is involved in taking an oath (Youth Justice and Criminal Evidence Act 1999, s 55(2)).

**57.** Section 114(1) of the Criminal Justice Act 2003 provides that a statement not made in oral evidence in the proceedings is only admissible as evidence of any matter stated if it comes within one of the exceptions to the rule against hearsay. Section 115(2) defines statement as 'any representation of fact or opinion made by a person by whatever means'. As a photograph is not a representation made by a person but simply the product of a mechanical process, it is not caught by the hearsay rule. Therefore, [A] is incorrect. [C] is incorrect because of the ruling of the Court of Appeal in *R v Cook* [1987] 1 All ER 1049, that inter alia, sketches and photographs, are in a class of their own to which the rule against previous consistent statements is not applicable. [D] is therefore correct. On the particular facts, see also *R v Dodson*; *R v Williams* (1984) 79 Cr App R 220, CA, where it was held that photographs taken by security cameras installed at a building society office at which an armed robbery was attempted, were admissible, being relevant to the issues of whether an offence was committed and, if so, who committed it. [B] is incorrect because although a document, for the purposes of the Criminal Justice Act 2003, s 117 is defined as 'anything in which information of any description is recorded' and therefore could arguably include a photograph (s 134(1)), the information contained in the photograph cannot be said to have been supplied by a person who had 'personal knowledge of the matters dealt with' as required by s 117(2)(b).

**58.** [B] is correct because the statement is evidence of a matter to which Tom could have testified if he had given evidence and Tom is dead (Criminal Justice Act 2003, s 116(1)(a) and (2)(a)). [A] is incorrect because the Police and Criminal Evidence Act 1984, s 76, which governs the admissibility of confessions in criminal cases, only admits 'a confession made by an accused person' (s 76(1)). [C] is incorrect because the statement was clearly not made in circumstances of such spontaneity or involvement in the event, ie the murder, that the possibility of concoction can be disregarded (see *Ratten v R* [1972] AC 378, PC etc). [D] is incorrect because the statement was not contained in a document (s 117(1) of the 2003 Act) nor was it created or received by a person in the course of a trade, business, profession etc (s 117(2)(a)).

**59.** [B] is correct because the statement is admissible original evidence, ie evidence tendered not as evidence of any matter stated in it but for some other relevant evidential purpose, namely to show what Robin, who heard it, thought or believed, which has an obvious relevance to his defence (see *Subramaniam v Public Prosecutor* [1956] 1 WLR 965). The relevant purpose of the evidence is to establish that

Robin was told the goods were not stolen, from which the jury *may* infer that he believed they were not stolen. [A] is incorrect because the event in question, the purchase of a video, can hardly be said to have been so unusual, startling or dramatic as to have dominated the thoughts of the neighbour and given him or her no real opportunity for reasoned reflection (see per Lord Ackner in *R v Andrews* [1957] 1 All ER 513, HL, at pp 520–1). [C] and [D] are incorrect because although the statement could be tendered for the truth of its contents the effect of the formal admission made on his behalf is that whether or not the recorder was stolen is no longer a fact in issue and therefore evidence on that matter is not relevant (Criminal Justice Act 1967, s 10).

**60.** In *R v Lucas* [1981] QB 720, it was held that to be capable of amounting to corroboration (i) the lie must be deliberate (ii) it must relate to a material issue (iii) the motive for it must be a realisation of guilt and a fear of the truth and (iv) it must clearly be shown to be a lie by admission or by evidence from an independent witness, ie a witness other than the witness requiring corroboration or a warning. There is no requirement that the lie should be in writing or otherwise recorded in documentary form. [B] is therefore the correct answer.

**61.** (i) is incorrect because a confession may be excluded under the Police and Criminal Evidence Act 1984, s 76(2)(b) where there is not even a suspicion of impropriety (see per Lord Lane CJ in *R v Fulling* [1987] 2 All ER 65, CA and, eg, *R v Harvey* [1988] Crim LR 241, CC). (ii) is correct because the test of reliability under s 76(2)(b) is hypothetical: the test is not whether the actual confession was untruthful or inaccurate, but whether whatever was said or done was, in the circumstances existing at the time, likely to have rendered any such confession unreliable. Thus although the test in s 76 cannot be satisfied by postulating some entirely different confession, the word 'any' in s 76(2)(b) must be understood as indicating 'any such' or 'such a' confession as the accused made (see *R v Barry* (1991) 95 Cr App R 384, CA and *Re Proulx* [2001] 1 All ER 57, CA). [C] is therefore the correct answer.

**62.** (i) is incorrect, because under the Police and Criminal Evidence Act 1984, s 76(2), the defence may raise the question of admissibility merely by making a 'representation' to the court that the confession was or may have been obtained by the methods described. The holding of a voir dire is thus not conditional upon evidence in support of such a representation. (ii) is incorrect because under s 76(2), a confession obtained by oppression will be excluded 'notwithstanding that it may be true'. [A] is therefore the correct answer.

**63.** The statement is hearsay because it will be adduced to prove the truth of the matters stated in it (the registration number of the Ford Escort). [D] is therefore incorrect. Section 117 is one of the statutory exceptions to the rule against hearsay in criminal proceedings. However, it only applies to statements contained in a document. [C] is therefore incorrect. Under s 116 evidence of a statement not made in oral evidence in the proceedings is admissible as evidence of any matter stated if oral evidence given in the proceedings by the person who made the statement would be admissible as evidence of that matter, the person who made the statement (the relevant person) is identified to the court's satisfaction and the relevant person is unavailable as a witness because, inter alia, he or she cannot be found although such steps as is reasonably practicable to take to find him have been taken. [B] is therefore correct and [A] incorrect.

**64.** The prosecution would not be relying on the piece of paper as evidence of any matter stated (ie, to prove that Brian was cool). Moreover, it is doubtful whether one of Brian's purposes in making the statement was to cause another person to believe that the matter stated was true (see ss 114(1) and 115(3) of the Criminal Justice Act 2003 and the case of *R v Lydon (Sean)* [1987] Crim LR 407). As a result the evidence is not hearsay and so answers [B] to [D] are incorrect. The piece of paper would be admissible as real evidence that would tend to prove the existence of one of the facts in issue, namely identification. [A] is therefore correct.

**65.** [C] is correct (and [A] and [B] incorrect) because in *R v Turnbull* [1977] QB 224, Lord Widgery CJ held that whenever the case against an accused depends wholly or substantially on the correctness of one or more identifications of the accused, which the defence allege to be mistaken, and in the judgment of the judge the quality of the identifying evidence is poor, he or she should direct an acquittal unless there is other evidence, which need not be corroboration in the strict sense, which goes to support the correctness of the identification. As to [D], a judge should not direct a jury that he would have withdrawn the case from them had he thought that there was insufficient identification evidence, because the jury may thereby mistakenly conclude that the evidence is sufficiently strong for them to convict (see *R v Smith and Doe* (1986) 85 Cr App R 197, CA and *R v Akaidere* [1990] Crim LR 808, CA).

**66.** The prosecution wish to adduce the woman's statement to prove that Dave was cycling away from the factory shortly after the fire started. The evidential value of the statement lies in the fact that the 'matter stated' is true. Section 115 of the Criminal Justice Act 2003 provides that a statement will only be hearsay where the purpose or one of the purposes of the maker of the statement appears to have been (a) to cause another person to believe the matter stated or (b) to cause another person to act on the basis that the matter is as stated. [B] is therefore correct and [C] incorrect. [D] is incorrect because the word 'only' is too restrictive: it will be hearsay if she intended another person to believe the matter or to cause someone other than Tegid to act on the basis that the matter was true. The fact that Tegid can give first-hand evidence of the statement does not prevent it from being hearsay, it only means that it is not multiple hearsay. [A] is therefore incorrect.

**67.** The facts clearly fall within the Criminal Justice and Public Order Act 1994, s 34(1): evidence has been given that Adam, on being questioned about the offence, failed to mention any of the facts relied on in his defence, being facts which, the parties agree, in the circumstances existing at the time he could reasonably have been expected to have mentioned. Therefore s 34(2) applies and the statements in (i) and (ii) are both accurate: see s 34(2)(c) and (d) respectively. The statement in (iii) is also accurate (see s 38(3)). [D] is therefore the correct answer.

**68.** [D] is correct (and [A], [B] and [C] incorrect) because where the jury can form their own opinion about a particular matter without the assistance of an expert, that matter being within their own knowledge and experience, expert opinion evidence is inadmissible because unnecessary (per Lawton LJ in *R v Turner* [1975] QB 834 at p 841). Thus expert psychiatric evidence is generally inadmissible on the question of *mens rea*, credibility, provocation or the reliability of a confession (although it is a practical necessity in order to establish insanity or diminished responsibility, and may be admissible on the question of *mens rea* or the reliability of a confession if the accused suffers from a mental illness). Compare the facts with those of *R v Turner*.

**69.** [B] is correct (and [C] and [D] are incorrect) because under the Police and Criminal Evidence Act 1984, s 67(9), the Codes apply not only to police officers, but also to other persons 'charged with the duty of investigating offences or charging offenders'; and whether a person satisfies this test is a question of fact in each case (per Watkins LJ in *R v Seelig* [1991] 4 All ER 429, CA, at p 439) or, more accurately, a question of mixed law and fact, involving an examination of the statute, contract or other authority under which a person carries out his functions, as well as a consideration of his actual work (*R v Bayliss* (1994) 98 Cr App R 235, CA and *R v Smith* (1994) 99 Cr App R 233, CA). As to [A], Naomi's questioning could have been an interview, which is defined as the questioning of a person regarding his involvement or suspected involvement in a criminal offence which is required to be carried out under caution: see ss 10.1 and 11.1A, Code C.

**70.** The facts of the case fall within the Criminal Justice and Public Order Act 1994, s 36(1)(a) and (b): the arresting officer reasonably believed that the condition of the clothing (see s 36(3)) was attributable to George's participation in the commission of the offence, and he informed George of his belief and asked him to account for the condition of his clothing, but George refused to do so. Prima facie, therefore, (a) the court, in deciding whether there is a case to answer, and (b) the court or jury, in deciding whether the accused is guilty of the offence charged, may draw proper inferences from the refusal: s 36(2). However, s 36(4) provides that s 36(1) and (2) do not apply unless the accused was told in ordinary language by the constable, when making the request, what the effect would be if he failed or refused to comply with it. [C] is therefore the correct answer.

# APPENDIX 5

## CIVIL LITIGATION SYLLABUS

High Court and county court jurisdiction.
Computation of time and non-compliance with rules of court.
Commencement of proceedings.
Pre-action protocols.
Statements of case and service.
Parties, joinder, representative actions, consolidation of actions, intervening, interpleader.
Third party (Part 20) procedure and contribution notices.
Procedure on interim applications.
Service outside the jurisdiction with and without permission.
Judgments in default.
Summary judgments and interim payments.
Interim injunctions, freezing injunctions and search orders.
Disclosure and inspection of documents.
*Norwich Pharmacal* orders; pre-action disclosure under SCA 1981, s 33(2); disclosure against non-parties under SCA 1981, s 34(2); orders for the inspection of property including orders under SCA 1981, s 34(3) and SCA 1981, s 33(1); interim delivery up of goods.
Requests for further information.
Limitation.
Amendment of statements of case, including amendment after the expiry of the limitation period.
Renewal of process.
Security for costs.
Part 36 payments and Part 36 offers.
Provisional damages.
Directions, track allocation and case management.
Striking out, sanctions, stays, discontinuance.
Experts, including obtaining facilities for examination, directions, joint experts, exchange of reports, procedure at trial.

Witness statements including exchange, procedure at trial and witness summaries.
Hearsay in civil proceedings including hearsay notices.
Notices to admit and prove.
Listing for trial.
Preliminary issues, witnesses, trial procedure.
References to the European Court.
Funding of litigation, public funding, conditional fee agreements and costs.
Judgments, consent orders, *Tomlin* orders, unless orders.
Enforcement.
Appeals.

## CRIMINAL LITIGATION AND SENTENCING SYLLABUS

*Preliminary Matters*

Police powers of arrest; detention at a police station under the Police and Criminal Evidence Act; access to legal advice; Codes of Practice issued under PACE 1984; 'serious arrestable offences'; charges; issue of process at Magistrates' Courts; Criminal Defence Service.

*Remands and Bail*

Distinguishing between simple adjournments and remands; situations where a remand must be used; duration of remands; general right to bail; attaching conditions to release on bail; sureties and forfeiture; applying for bail; limit on number of applications; appeals to or variations by a Crown Court judge; custody time limits.

*Mode of Trial*

Classification of offences; determination of mode of trial including the plea before venue procedure; special provisions for criminal damage; advance information; Criminal Justice Act 1988, ss 40 and 41.

*Summary Trial*

Procedure at trial of a charge or summons; joint trial of separate informations; proceeding in the accused's absence; guilty pleas by post; committals for sentence to the Crown Court.

*Transfer of either-way cases to the Crown Court*

Transfer under Crime and Disorder Act 1998, s 51; voluntary bills of indictment.

*Juveniles and the Courts*

Who is a juvenile; the work of the Youth Court; which courts can try juveniles; which courts can pass sentence on juveniles; limits on sentencing powers; committal for trial; publicity and public access; use of reprimands and warnings by police.

*Appeals from the Magistrates' Court*

Appeals to the Crown Court; applications to the Divisional Court for judicial review or appeals by way of case stated; appeal to the House of Lords from the Divisional Court.

*Crown Court: Pre-trial Issues*

Disclosure; preparatory hearings; pre-trial hearings; plea and directions hearings.

*Indictments, Pleas and Crown Court Preliminaries*

The structure of an indictment; separate counts and duplicity; joining several counts and accused in one indictment; amending indictments; use of alternative counts; pleas by the accused; fitness to plead; change of plea; plea to an alternative offence; abuse of process.

*Jury Trials*

The sequence of a jury trial; absence of accused from court; when opening or closing speeches may be made; seeing the judge about plea or sentence; empanelling a jury; procedure where admissibility of evidence is disputed; making a formal admission; submission of no case to answer; functions of judge and jury; contents of a summing-up; directions to a jury after their retirement; discharge of jurors; the verdict of the jury; majority verdicts; verdict of guilty of an alternative offence.

*Appeals to the Court of Appeal*

Certificate from the trial judge; getting leave to appeal from a single judge of the Court of Appeal; grounds of appeal against conviction – Criminal Appeal Act 1968, s 2; appeal against sentence; appeals on fresh evidence; powers of the single judge; powers of the Court of Appeal; directions for loss of time; references by the Attorney-General; appeal to the House of Lords; reference to the European Court of Justice.

*Sentencing and Costs*

Basic sentencing powers of the Magistrates' and Crown Courts; sentencing procedure in both the Magistrates' and Crown Court;

statutory principles and guidelines cases; maximum and minimum for common types of sentence or order; when such sentences or orders can be used; costs orders; anti-social behaviour orders.

## EVIDENCE SYLLABUS

Facts open to proof or disproof.
Formal admissions.
Judicial notice.
Basic concepts: relevance, admissibility, weight and sufficiency.
Varieties of evidence.
Discretion.
Functions of judge and jury.
Burden and standard of proof.
Presumptions (including conflicting presumptions, but in outline only).
Witnesses: attendance of witnesses and procedural issues, sworn and unsworn evidence and competence and compellability.
Examination-in-chief including leading questions, refreshing memory, previous consistent statements and unfavourable and hostile witnesses.
Cross-examination including liability to cross-examination, cross-examination on documents, cross-examination as to credit, the character of the complainant on charges of rape, previous inconsistent statements, and the rule of finality of answers to collateral questions and exceptions thereto.
Re-examination.
Similar fact evidence.
Character evidence.
The hearsay rule including its scope, original evidence, implied assertions, negative hearsay and statements produced by calculators etc.
Statutory and common law exceptions to the hearsay rule, including the relevant Civil Procedure Rules.
Confessions, including all relevant sections of the Police and Criminal Evidence Act 1984 and the Codes of Practice.
Illegally and improperly obtained evidence.
Inferences from accused's conduct, lies, failure to comply with the duty of disclosure, silence, failure or refusal to account for objects, substances, marks or presence at a particular place and refusal to consent to the taking of samples.

Opinion evidence, including the relevant Civil Procedure Rules and Crown Court Rules.

Judgments as evidence of the facts on which they are based including exceptions to the rule in *Hollington v Hewthorn*, convictions of the accused and convictions of persons other than the accused.

Corroboration and warnings required as a matter of practice.

Identification.

Privilege including privacy and confidential relationships.

Public interest immunity (in outline only).

Documentary evidence.

Real evidence.

# ANSWER SHEET

Read the instructions before you start to fill in the answers.

INSTRUCTIONS

1. Use the HB pencil provided.
2. Fill in the boxes like this [▬] not like this [✓] [✗] [✓]
3. Fill in the boxes to indicate the subjects and whether this is a resit.
4. Write in your candidate number and the examination date in the spaces provided **and** fill in the boxes below.
5. Write your name and signature in the spaces provided.
6. Each question has four possible answers lettered A to D. Read all four answers **in full** before making a selection. Select the answer which you think is correct/best and indicate it on the answer sheet by filling in the appropriate box.
7. If you fill in two or more boxes in any question, that question will carry no mark.
8. Erase all mistakes thoroughly using the eraser provided.

**SUBJECT**

| | |
|---|---|
| Evidence & Civil Litigation | [ ] |
| Evidence & Criminal Litigation | [ ] |
| Is this a resit? Yes | [ ] |
| No | [ ] |

**CANDIDATE NUMBER**

| | | | |
|---|---|---|---|
| [0] | [0] | [0] | [0] |
| [1] | [1] | [1] | [1] |
| [2] | [2] | [2] | [2] |
| [3] | [3] | [3] | [3] |
| [4] | [4] | [4] | [4] |
| [5] | [5] | [5] | [5] |
| [6] | [6] | [6] | [6] |
| [7] | [7] | [7] | [7] |
| [8] | [8] | [8] | [8] |
| [9] | [9] | [9] | [9] |

**DATE OF EXAM**

| DAY | | MONTH | | YEAR | |
|---|---|---|---|---|---|
| [0] | [0] | [0] | [0] | [0] | [0] |
| [1] | [1] | [1] | [1] | [1] | [1] |
| [2] | [2] | | [2] | [2] | [2] |
| [3] | [3] | | [3] | [3] | [3] |
| | [4] | | [4] | [4] | [4] |
| | [5] | | [5] | [5] | [5] |
| | [6] | | [6] | [6] | [6] |
| | [7] | | [7] | [7] | [7] |
| | [8] | | [8] | [8] | [8] |
| | [9] | | [9] | [9] | [9] |

| | | | | | | | |
|---|---|---|---|---|---|---|---|
| 1 | [A] [B] [C] [D] | 21 | [A] [B] [C] [D] | 41 | [A] [B] [C] [D] | 61 | [A] [B] [C] [D] |
| 2 | [A] [B] [C] [D] | 22 | [A] [B] [C] [D] | 42 | [A] [B] [C] [D] | 62 | [A] [B] [C] [D] |
| 3 | [A] [B] [C] [D] | 23 | [A] [B] [C] [D] | 43 | [A] [B] [C] [D] | 63 | [A] [B] [C] [D] |
| 4 | [A] [B] [C] [D] | 24 | [A] [B] [C] [D] | 44 | [A] [B] [C] [D] | 64 | [A] [B] [C] [D] |
| 5 | [A] [B] [C] [D] | 25 | [A] [B] [C] [D] | 45 | [A] [B] [C] [D] | 65 | [A] [B] [C] [D] |
| 6 | [A] [B] [C] [D] | 26 | [A] [B] [C] [D] | 46 | [A] [B] [C] [D] | 66 | [A] [B] [C] [D] |
| 7 | [A] [B] [C] [D] | 27 | [A] [B] [C] [D] | 47 | [A] [B] [C] [D] | 67 | [A] [B] [C] [D] |
| 8 | [A] [B] [C] [D] | 28 | [A] [B] [C] [D] | 48 | [A] [B] [C] [D] | 68 | [A] [B] [C] [D] |
| 9 | [A] [B] [C] [D] | 29 | [A] [B] [C] [D] | 49 | [A] [B] [C] [D] | 69 | [A] [B] [C] [D] |
| 10 | [A] [B] [C] [D] | 30 | [A] [B] [C] [D] | 50 | [A] [B] [C] [D] | 70 | [A] [B] [C] [D] |
| 11 | [A] [B] [C] [D] | 31 | [A] [B] [C] [D] | 51 | [A] [B] [C] [D] | 71 | [A] [B] [C] [D] |
| 12 | [A] [B] [C] [D] | 32 | [A] [B] [C] [D] | 52 | [A] [B] [C] [D] | 72 | [A] [B] [C] [D] |
| 13 | [A] [B] [C] [D] | 33 | [A] [B] [C] [D] | 53 | [A] [B] [C] [D] | 73 | [A] [B] [C] [D] |
| 14 | [A] [B] [C] [D] | 34 | [A] [B] [C] [D] | 54 | [A] [B] [C] [D] | 74 | [A] [B] [C] [D] |
| 15 | [A] [B] [C] [D] | 35 | [A] [B] [C] [D] | 55 | [A] [B] [C] [D] | 75 | [A] [B] [C] [D] |
| 16 | [A] [B] [C] [D] | 36 | [A] [B] [C] [D] | 56 | [A] [B] [C] [D] | 76 | [A] [B] [C] [D] |
| 17 | [A] [B] [C] [D] | 37 | [A] [B] [C] [D] | 57 | [A] [B] [C] [D] | 77 | [A] [B] [C] [D] |
| 18 | [A] [B] [C] [D] | 38 | [A] [B] [C] [D] | 58 | [A] [B] [C] [D] | 78 | [A] [B] [C] [D] |
| 19 | [A] [B] [C] [D] | 39 | [A] [B] [C] [D] | 59 | [A] [B] [C] [D] | 79 | [A] [B] [C] [D] |
| 20 | [A] [B] [C] [D] | 40 | [A] [B] [C] [D] | 60 | [A] [B] [C] [D] | 80 | [A] [B] [C] [D] |

Have you filled in correctly the spaces provided for your name, subject, candidate number and exam date?

SURNAME & INITIALS

SIGNATURE

# ANSWER SHEET

Read the instructions before you start to fill in the answers.

INSTRUCTIONS

1. Use the HB pencil provided.
2. Fill in the boxes like this [▬] not like this [/] [✗] [✓]
3. Fill in the boxes to indicate the subjects and whether this is a resit.
4. Write in your candidate number and the examination date in the spaces provided **and** fill in the boxes below.
5. Write your name and signature in the spaces provided.
6. Each question has four possible answers lettered A to D. Read all four answers **in full** before making a selection. Select the answer which you think is correct/best and indicate it on the answer sheet by filling in the appropriate box.
7. If you fill in two or more boxes in any question, that question will carry no mark.
8. Erase all mistakes thoroughly using the eraser provided.

**SUBJECT**

| | |
|---|---|
| Evidence & Civil Litigation | [ ] |
| Evidence & Criminal Litigation | [ ] |
| Is this a resit? | Yes [ ] No [ ] |

**CANDIDATE NUMBER**

| | | | |
|---|---|---|---|
| [0] | [0] | [0] | [0] |
| [1] | [1] | [1] | [1] |
| [2] | [2] | [2] | [2] |
| [3] | [3] | [3] | [3] |
| [4] | [4] | [4] | [4] |
| [5] | [5] | [5] | [5] |
| [6] | [6] | [6] | [6] |
| [7] | [7] | [7] | [7] |
| [8] | [8] | [8] | [8] |
| [9] | [9] | [9] | [9] |

**DATE OF EXAM**

| DAY | | MONTH | | YEAR | |
|---|---|---|---|---|---|
| | | | | | |
| [0] | [0] | [0] | [0] | [0] | [0] |
| [1] | [1] | [1] | [1] | [1] | [1] |
| [2] | [2] | | [2] | [2] | [2] |
| [3] | [3] | | [3] | [3] | [3] |
| | [4] | | [4] | [4] | [4] |
| | [5] | | [5] | [5] | [5] |
| | [6] | | [6] | [6] | [6] |
| | [7] | | [7] | [7] | [7] |
| | [8] | | [8] | [8] | [8] |
| | [9] | | [9] | [9] | [9] |

| | | | | | | | |
|---|---|---|---|---|---|---|---|
| 1 | [A] [B] [C] [D] | 21 | [A] [B] [C] [D] | 41 | [A] [B] [C] [D] | 61 | [A] [B] [C] [D] |
| 2 | [A] [B] [C] [D] | 22 | [A] [B] [C] [D] | 42 | [A] [B] [C] [D] | 62 | [A] [B] [C] [D] |
| 3 | [A] [B] [C] [D] | 23 | [A] [B] [C] [D] | 43 | [A] [B] [C] [D] | 63 | [A] [B] [C] [D] |
| 4 | [A] [B] [C] [D] | 24 | [A] [B] [C] [D] | 44 | [A] [B] [C] [D] | 64 | [A] [B] [C] [D] |
| 5 | [A] [B] [C] [D] | 25 | [A] [B] [C] [D] | 45 | [A] [B] [C] [D] | 65 | [A] [B] [C] [D] |
| 6 | [A] [B] [C] [D] | 26 | [A] [B] [C] [D] | 46 | [A] [B] [C] [D] | 66 | [A] [B] [C] [D] |
| 7 | [A] [B] [C] [D] | 27 | [A] [B] [C] [D] | 47 | [A] [B] [C] [D] | 67 | [A] [B] [C] [D] |
| 8 | [A] [B] [C] [D] | 28 | [A] [B] [C] [D] | 48 | [A] [B] [C] [D] | 68 | [A] [B] [C] [D] |
| 9 | [A] [B] [C] [D] | 29 | [A] [B] [C] [D] | 49 | [A] [B] [C] [D] | 69 | [A] [B] [C] [D] |
| 10 | [A] [B] [C] [D] | 30 | [A] [B] [C] [D] | 50 | [A] [B] [C] [D] | 70 | [A] [B] [C] [D] |
| 11 | [A] [B] [C] [D] | 31 | [A] [B] [C] [D] | 51 | [A] [B] [C] [D] | 71 | [A] [B] [C] [D] |
| 12 | [A] [B] [C] [D] | 32 | [A] [B] [C] [D] | 52 | [A] [B] [C] [D] | 72 | [A] [B] [C] [D] |
| 13 | [A] [B] [C] [D] | 33 | [A] [B] [C] [D] | 53 | [A] [B] [C] [D] | 73 | [A] [B] [C] [D] |
| 14 | [A] [B] [C] [D] | 34 | [A] [B] [C] [D] | 54 | [A] [B] [C] [D] | 74 | [A] [B] [C] [D] |
| 15 | [A] [B] [C] [D] | 35 | [A] [B] [C] [D] | 55 | [A] [B] [C] [D] | 75 | [A] [B] [C] [D] |
| 16 | [A] [B] [C] [D] | 36 | [A] [B] [C] [D] | 56 | [A] [B] [C] [D] | 76 | [A] [B] [C] [D] |
| 17 | [A] [B] [C] [D] | 37 | [A] [B] [C] [D] | 57 | [A] [B] [C] [D] | 77 | [A] [B] [C] [D] |
| 18 | [A] [B] [C] [D] | 38 | [A] [B] [C] [D] | 58 | [A] [B] [C] [D] | 78 | [A] [B] [C] [D] |
| 19 | [A] [B] [C] [D] | 39 | [A] [B] [C] [D] | 59 | [A] [B] [C] [D] | 79 | [A] [B] [C] [D] |
| 20 | [A] [B] [C] [D] | 40 | [A] [B] [C] [D] | 60 | [A] [B] [C] [D] | 80 | [A] [B] [C] [D] |

Have you filled in correctly the spaces provided for your name, subject, candidate number and exam date?

SURNAME & INITIALS

SIGNATURE